Aiming to Win

Aiming to Win

An Evidence-Informed Approach for Law Enforcement

Training in Target-Focused Shooting

Leon Reha

ABOUT THE AUTHOR

Leon brings over twenty years of law enforcement experience and training expertise to his work, with a distinguished career spanning operational policing in the U.S. and the U.K., serving in specialized roles, and leadership of a large-scale law enforcement training program. His career started with the London Metropolitan Police in 2001, where he served as a patrol officer before being selected for the elite Specialist Firearms Command. During his tenure, he completed hundreds of successful deployments with a flawless record of conduct and safety.

Now based in the United States, Leon has established himself as a leading authority in law enforcement training methodology. From 2018 to 2024, he served as the Firearms Training Coordinator for a state Public Safety Academy, overseeing all firearms training programs. In this leadership role, he trained and led a team of firearms instructors and served as the department's subject matter expert and liaison for more than 200 law enforcement agencies across the state.

Leon's achievements include developing and implementing research-based curricula grounded in adult learning principles and long-term skill retention. He designed comprehensive, multi-stage, evidence-informed assessment processes and created instructor development courses for the department. His innovative approach aligned training protocols with operational needs and human performance factors, earning him multiple commendations for performance excellence and program innovation.

Leon's credentials demonstrate his dedication to training excellence and evidence-based methodology. As an Advanced Force Science Specialist, he applies cutting-edge research and scientific principles to tactical training, integrating psychological research and behavioral science into practical instruction that challenges traditional approaches. His role as a SIG SAUER Academy instructor—one of the world's leading firearms training institutions—demonstrates his recognition among industry leaders as a subject-matter expert. At SIG SAUER, he successfully led the redesign of advanced firearms courses and developed new, research-informed training models to improve effectiveness, efficiency, and consistency.

His international perspective and extensive teaching experience have made him a sought-after speaker and collaborator. He has delivered training across the U.S. and internationally, adapting proven methodologies to diverse operational environments. His expertise is recognized through memberships in the International Law Enforcement Educators and Trainers Association (ILEETA) and the American Psychological Association (APA), reflecting his commitment to both tactical excellence and the psychological foundations of effective training.

His contributions extend beyond the classroom through published articles in respected industry outlets such as Police1, the ILEETA Journal, and The Firearms Instructor. This unique combination of elite operational experience, proven leadership in large-scale training programs, and dedication to research-based methodology positions Leon as a leading authority in evidence-based training that emphasizes effectiveness over tradition.

Table of Contents

PREFACE

The methodical crack of gunfire shatters the sterile silence of the shooting range as officers line up in perfect formation, squinting through sights at static paper targets twenty-five yards downrange. Each shot is slow and deliberate, measured, scored. The instructor calls time, and officers walk forward to examine their neat, tight groupings with satisfaction. Another qualification passed. Another box checked. Yet somewhere in their minds, a troubling question lingers, and it should; when the moment of truth arrives, when they face a deadly threat in a dimly lit alley, with fractions of a second to react and lives hanging in the balance, will any of this matter?

This book bridges the chasm between traditional marksmanship training and the brutal reality of close, fast, and devastating armed encounters in law enforcement. For too long, our profession has clung to training methodologies prioritizing precision over speed, perfection over practicality, and test scores over tactical effectiveness. We have created a generation of officers who can generate satisfactory groups on paper but struggle to comprehend why their finely tuned range marksmanship skills appear insufficient when faced with the chaos of a real gunfight.

Proximity and life-threatening fear fundamentally alter both physiological and psychological processes. Stress-induced physiological arousal transforms how decisions are made, and skills are executed. The techniques professionals are trained in should reflect the reality of operational application. This text is written primarily for law enforcement firearms instructors, whose students must perform under conditions where saving lives, not scoring points, is the metric that matters. While competitive and recreational shooters may benefit from these principles, this work focuses on those who protect life under extreme duress, and the trainers who help them prepare to do so. The purpose of this book is threefold:

I.   Provide a comprehensive historical foundation for target-focused shooting techniques

II. Challenge the entrenched dogma that has divorced police firearms training from operational reality

III. Support this paradigm shift with rigorous, peer-reviewed research

This book traces the evolution of point shooting and target-focused techniques from their life-saving origins, through their adaptation to law enforcement and military contexts, examining when and where these methods prove most relevant and effective.

More critically, this book confronts an uncomfortable truth within law enforcement training culture: we have become obsessed with slowly passing tests rather than rapidly winning fights. Our qualification courses have become elaborate exercises in marksmanship that bear little resemblance to the close-quarters, high-stress encounters officers actually face. We have prioritized the ability to administratively place holes in two-dimensional paper products over the capacity to rapidly engage dynamic threats while under extreme duress.

Law enforcement firearms trainers are the gatekeepers of competency, shaping how officers prepare for the ultimate test of their profession. The scope deliberately focuses on challenging these trainers to expand their understanding beyond traditional marksmanship fundamentals. Creating small groups at extended distances, while demonstrating certain technical skills, does not translate to fighting effectiveness when an officer has milliseconds to react to a life-threatening situation at arm's length.

The content boundaries encompass the historical development of target-focused shooting, the physiological and psychological factors that govern performance under extreme stress, and the tactical applications most relevant to law enforcement encounters. This book does not attempt to replace fundamental marksmanship training entirely, but rather to contextualize when and how different aiming techniques should be employed based on situational demands.

The structure of this book follows a logical progression intended to build understanding and systematically challenge assumptions. We start with the historical origins of target-focused shooting, tracing its development and eventual adoption by innovative law enforcement agencies. This historical foundation establishes credibility and demonstrates that these techniques are not revolutionary concepts, but rather time-tested methods that range-based training traditions have overshadowed.

Subsequent chapters investigate the scientific basis for target-focused shooting through peer-reviewed research in human performance and motor learning. This empirical foundation transforms what has long been forgotten into a legitimate, research-backed training methodology. We examine the neurological realities of high-stress encounters, the shifts in attentional capacity, and the limitations in visual processing that make traditional sight alignment techniques impractical or physiologically impossible in some situations.

The book then addresses the practical application of these concepts through foundational training methodology, recommendations, and implementation strategies. Each chapter is designed to equip trainers with both theoretical understanding and practical tools they can reference and immediately integrate into their programs. This book provides trainers with the evidence and knowledge necessary to advocate for more realistic and effective training methodologies within their organizations.

The ultimate goal is to prepare officers not only to pass qualification courses but also to succeed in the violent encounters that represent the highest stakes of their profession. The gap between range performance and street effectiveness has cost lives. It's time to close that gap.

CHAPTER 1 - INTRODUCTION

How to Use This Book

This book is structured to take you on a journey from historical foundation to practical application. Unlike typical firearms training manuals that focus primarily on technique, this work integrates historical context, scientific research, and practical training methods to provide a comprehensive understanding of target-focused shooting for law enforcement applications.

The book is organized into distinct sections that build upon each other:

Historical Foundation - Understanding the origins of target-focused shooting and its development provides crucial context for its modern application. The techniques you'll learn aren't experimental concepts—they're time-tested methods refined by legendary shooters and combat veterans.

Research and Evidence - Before diving into the technique, we examine the gap between traditional training and operational reality, then explore peer-reviewed research that validates target-focused approaches. This scientific foundation transforms what some dismiss as unaimed shooting into an evidence-based training methodology.

Human Performance Factors - Vision and attention are the foundations of target-focused shooting. Understanding how your visual system works and how attention functions under stress is essential for proper technique development and training design.

Tactical Application - The book addresses when and where target-focused shooting is most relevant, helping you understand that this isn't a replacement for all shooting techniques, but rather the right aiming tool for specific situations.

Training Implementation - Finally, we cover how learning is most effectively achieved and how to train these skills, from foundational concepts to advanced applications.

What This Book Is Not

This is not another marksmanship manual focused on creating tight groups at extended distances. This book addresses explicitly close-quarters, high-stress encounters where traditional sight alignment becomes impractical or impossible. While precision shooting skills remain essential, they represent only one part of a complete shooting skill set.

This book does not advocate abandoning fundamental shooting principles. Instead, it shows how to adapt those principles to the realities of law enforcement encounters where proximity, time pressure, and life-threatening stress fundamentally alter how shooting skills must be applied.

Understanding "It Is All Aiming"

One of the most important concepts you'll encounter here is that target-focused shooting is not "un-aimed" fire. The human body is a sophisticated pointing instrument, and target-focused techniques harness this skill that has been honed over a lifetime while working within the constraints imposed by high-stress encounters. Understanding this aiming distinction is crucial for both proper technique development and overcoming institutional resistance to these methods.

Under life-threatening fear, human attention narrows dramatically. Our brains direct our attention to the immediate threat, not the object held in our hands, certainly not the tiny bumps on top of it. This biological reality, hardwired into our survival mechanisms, often conflicts with traditional firearms training that emphasizes sight use above all else.

For two centuries, while sighting systems on handguns have evolved significantly, the human operating them remains essentially unchanged. However, formal firearms instruction continues to fixate on sight alignment, sight picture, and front sight focus. "Slow and steady wins the race" approaches dominate training manuals and qualification courses. Somehow, scoring points on paper targets has become the primary focus for professionals who carry firearms not for sport, but for survival.

3

Armed professionals who carry firearms to defend themselves or others require training that acknowledges physiological realities. Traditional sighting techniques may prove inefficient and potentially fatal when facing an imminent threat at close quarters. If sight-focused shooting is all you have practiced, you may spend the last moments of your life searching for a sight picture that stress and proximity make impossible to acquire.

"Always" and "never" rarely apply in the dynamic, chaotic reality of lethal force encounters. Context must drive decision-making and technique selection. While aiming remains essential, multiple valid methods exist beyond traditional sighting. This book explores the often-overlooked and misunderstood non-sighted aiming process, specifically focusing on handgun application during time-compressed, close-quarters encounters.

Anyone who claims that sights are always required is wrong.

Anyone who tells you sights are never required is equally wrong.

The Evidence-Informed Approach

Throughout this book, practical recommendations are supported by peer-reviewed research from leading institutions and researchers in human performance, law enforcement training, and tactical studies. This scientific foundation accomplishes two critical objectives: it validates training methods that have often been dismissed as personal preference or opinion, and it provides the evidence necessary to advocate for program changes within your organization.

Key research areas you'll encounter include studies on officer movement under stress, decision-making in shoot/no-shoot scenarios, gaze control during high-pressure situations, and kinematic analysis of shooting performance in realistic encounters. This research transforms anecdotal observations into training doctrine supported by empirical evidence.

Vision and Attention: The Foundation

Before learning target-focused techniques, you must understand the physiological systems that make them work. The human visual system and attention mechanisms function very differently under extreme stress than they do in controlled training environments. Traditional training often ignores these realities, creating a disconnect between range performance and operational effectiveness.

The chapters on vision and attention provide an evidence-informed foundation for understanding why target-focused shooting works and when it's most appropriate. This knowledge is essential not only for developing proper technique but also for designing training that transfers effectively to real-world encounters.

Skill Types and Context-Driven Application

Target-focused shooting is most relevant in what motor learning research calls "open skill" environments—situations where conditions are unpredictable and responses must be adapted in real-time. Understanding when and where these techniques apply helps you avoid the mistake of trying to use the wrong tool for the job.

The danger zones identified through data analysis of law enforcement encounters reveal specific distance and time parameters where target-focused techniques provide tactical advantages over traditional marksmanship approaches. This isn't an opinion about where things could happen; it's a data-driven fact about where it does happen.

Training Philosophy

The training section of this book challenges conventional wisdom about skill development progression. Rather than treating target-focused shooting as an advanced technique to be learned after mastering traditional marksmanship, the evidence suggests these skills should be developed from the beginning of firearms training.

The training methods described here emphasize realistic skill development, techniques designed to withstand operational stress, and diagnostic applications that help identify when officers revert to ineffective techniques under pressure. The goal is skill acquisition, retention, and transfer under the conditions where these techniques are most needed.

Implementation Considerations

Introducing target-focused shooting into established training programs requires more than teaching new techniques. It requires challenging institutional assumptions about what constitutes effective firearms training. This book provides the methods, rationale, and evidence necessary to advocate for change within your organization.

Expect resistance. Traditional qualification courses, range design, and administrative policies often conflict with evidence-based training approaches. The historical precedent, scientific foundation, and practical results documented in this book provide the tools to source evidence necessary to overcome this resistance professionally and effectively.

Safety and Legal Considerations

All techniques and training methods described in this book must be implemented within appropriate safety protocols and institutional guidelines. Properly executed target-focused shooting enhances both speed and accuracy in relevant circumstances. However, like all firearms training, it must be conducted by qualified instructors in appropriate training environments. Officers trained in the application of these skills are better prepared to make accurate, accountable shots under the stress they may face.

Your Journey Forward

This book challenges you to examine your current training methods critically and honestly. It asks whether your training truly prepares officers for the encounters they may face, or whether it simply helps them pass qualification courses that bear little resemblance to operational reality.

The journey from traditional range-based training to comprehensive operational preparation is not always comfortable. It requires acknowledging that some long-held beliefs about firearms instruction may not serve our officers' best interests. But the stakes of law enforcement demand nothing less than training that genuinely prepares officers for the life-and-death decisions they may be called upon to make.

The historical figures profiled in this book faced similar challenges in their time—advocating for training methods that diverged from established doctrine because operational effectiveness required it. Their legacy offers inspiration and validation for continuing this evolution in law enforcement firearms training.

The question is not whether these methods work—the research and historical precedent demonstrate their effectiveness. The question is whether we have the professional courage to implement them despite institutional inertia and traditional thinking.

Your officers' lives, and the lives of those they protect, depend on getting this right.

CHAPTER 2 - A BRIEF HISTORY OF TARGET-FOCUSED SHOOTING

Let's start with some clarity on terminology. I will use the term "Target-focused shooting" (TFS) throughout the text. The same concept has been and continues to be described in several ways. No one term is more accurate than the other. I didn't invent the term TFS, but I chose it because it efficiently identifies and describes the technique. Simplicity is something I pursue relentlessly. Complicating things to exclude others or inflate your brilliance is not the mark of a true educator/trainer. It is far more inspiring when someone takes something potentially complicated and finds a way to make it accessible.

Other terms for this aiming technique are point shooting, kinesthetic shooting, index shooting, instinctive shooting, instinctive combat shooting, stance-directed fire, or reflexive shooting. Each term is usually associated with a particular trainer or proponent of the technique. There may be nuances in placement or position of body, foot, arm, or elbow that different groups affiliate with as *the* way to do it. There may also be other equally valid terms to describe the concept. The fact that I have not referenced them all is nothing worth reading into.

It is fascinating to see that modern research supports what we have long known to be valid and successful. We know far more about vision, attention, speed, decision-making, and learning than ever. What was once considered common sense based on experience now has decades of supporting research to validate it. There is no denying the technique's viability, yet it is feared, forgotten, or fundamentally misunderstood for some reason.

The first written reference I can locate specifically to target-focused shooting in contradiction of sight use with a handgun is a book called 'Helps and Hints how to Protect Life and Property.' The book was published in 1835, and the author was Lt. Col. Baron De Berenger. In his writing, De Berenger refers to sights being available on pistols and shares his disapproval that recreational target shooting is misconstrued as practice for using a pistol as a tool for combat.

This does not mean that target-focused shooting was invented at that time. Instead, this seems to be the beginning of a formal distinction between focusing on the target and focusing on the firearm's sights. Target-focused shooting existed well before De Berenger's writing, but his text shows that the debate between using sights or not was underway. Remarkably, almost 200 years later, this debate continues unresolved.

We humans have been hitting targets long before sights existed. Looking at what we wanted to hit was customary for thousands of years. Body parts do not come with sights, but we can effectively use fists, elbows, shoulders, knees, and feet to strike our opponents. Extensions of our bodies, like sticks, knives, swords, and clubs, allowed us to inflict injury on our opponents or prey without looking at anything except our opponents or prey. Projectiles, rocks, spears, and arrows all revolved around us, looking at what we wanted to hit and being able to keep further away from danger.

As we have progressed in our ability to maintain range from our targets, we have developed sighting systems to aid in that long-range engagement. We are trying to compare the extremes of firing projectiles around the planet to the exchange of gunfire at an arm's length. Our obsession with sighting systems has become an absolute concern regarding aiming handguns. It has not always been this way. It seems that someone rediscovered this "secret" technique of aiming without sights every few years. I cannot tell you why it is not the norm, but I can tell you that in the distances where people fight with handguns and especially where they lose while doing so, it is ideal to disregard the sights and leverage TFS.

The following are some of the authors and trainers who have been proponents of this aiming methodology over the last two centuries.

Lt. Col. Baron De Berenger

Lieutenant Colonel Charles Random Baron de Berenger (1772-1846) was a fascinating character in early 19th-century Britain. An inventor, award-winning shooter, and sought-after trainer, he made pioneering contributions to firearms design. In his younger years, he also achieved notoriety for involvement in a financial scandal, which earned him a year of incarceration (Credland, 2006).

De Berenger owned and operated Britain's first sports complex, 'The Stadium'. Patrons could engage in shooting, archery, fencing, wrestling, gymnastics, equestrian sports, swimming, sailing, cricket, golf, and exotic pursuits like javelin and boomerang throwing (Credland, 2006).

As well as being an entrepreneur and prolific inventor, his lasting legacy came from authorship. His 1835 book was based on letters he wrote to his son Augustus, providing guidance on everything from street safety to marksmanship instruction. In it, de Berenger clearly established his position on the sighted use of pistols in close quarters. It is safe to say he was not an advocate for sighted fire in these circumstances; he considered sight use slow, laborious, and entirely impractical for protection.

Self-defence requires rapid pistol shooting, and therefore precludes a deliberate aim along the barrel.

De Berenger recognized the overwhelming need for speed in close-quarters defensive circumstances. He explained how to aim by pointing without looking along the barrel. He also encouraged people to practice 'pointing' even without a pistol to build the skill. This guidance represents a crucial bridge between 18th-century dueling traditions and modern practical shooting methods.

His book is the earliest known comprehensive self-defense manual, and his insights into rapid, instinctive shooting techniques later gained widespread acceptance in military and law enforcement circles during the 20th century. De Berenger's technical innovations and forward-thinking approach to personal protection established him as a pivotal figure in the development of both firearms' technology and self-defense methodology.

James Butler Hickok

James Butler Hickok (1837-1876) was not perhaps the most famous gunfighter, but you may have heard his more common nickname, "Wild Bill" Hickok. Wild Bill was one of the deadliest Western gunfighters in history. Between July 1861 and October 1871, Hickok was involved in 7 separate gunfights and killed at least 7 of his opponents (O'Neal, 1983). Many years later, Col. Rex Applegate was researching Hickok (Col. Rex Applegate & Michael D. Janich, 1998), and he discovered a letter written by Hickok that was never mailed. In that letter, Hickok was answering the question, "How did you kill those men?" Hickok described his shooting technique like this: "I raised my hand to eye level, like pointing a finger, and fired." Essentially, that is how it has been done for centuries. The advent of sights and the obsession with pinpoint precision firing have deluded people into a false sense of what shooting a handgun to preserve life looks like.

Lt. Col. William Fairbairn

In the early 1900s, one of the most famous names in the realm of target-focused shooting came to the forefront. Lt. Col William Fairbairn was born in Hertfordshire, England, on February 28th, 1885. He joined the Marines when he was just 15 years old in 1901 (Robins et al., 2005). His discovery of target-focused shooting came to pass in Shanghai. He served as a member of the Shanghai Municipal Police from 1907 to 1940. Shanghai was one of the most dangerous places on the planet during that time, and its officers were regularly involved in exchanges of violence. They did not always prevail.

Early in his career, Fairbairn learned the inadequacy of the training he had received from his agency when he was almost killed by a gang that beat him unconscious in an alleyway (Robins et al., 2005). He resolved not only to learn a more practical way to fight and win, but he also wanted to share that training with his fellow officers. He worked tirelessly to build his combative skills. He finally convinced his senior officers to allow him to train the officers in a practical way that would enable them to succeed at their jobs rather than checking boxes on tests. He was a formidable hand-to-hand fighter but also had a forward-thinking approach to handgun use. When it came to shooting, he identified two areas required to prevail in close-quarter gun use:

- Extreme speed in both drawing and firing
- Instinctive as opposed to deliberate aim

Fairbairn advocated various handgun positions depending on distance. The further the target was from the shooter, the further forward from the body the gun was presented. This ranged from a single-handed presentation termed the "close hip" technique at 3 feet or less, all the way through to a two-handed presentation for a "long shot" at 30 feet or more.

Fairbairn condemned sights for short-range shooting. He is often portrayed as being anti-sight use, but he did not limit himself solely to a target-focused approach to aiming. He supported using two hands to grip and sights to aim for long-distance shots.

Fairbairn had great success training people in his 'new' system of handgun use, and the real-world results of the effort were identifiable in the operational use of the technique. Do not get me wrong; Fairbairn did not solve all problems. There was no fairytale ending to all crime and violence. However, the Shanghai police did improve their odds with the new technique, and Fairbairn detailed those stats in the book Shooting to Live with the One-Hand Gun, which he authored with his friend and teammate Eric Sykes.

Fairbairn wrote articles and traveled to various countries, observing, training, and teaching his techniques. In 1940, he was employed by the British Secret Service to train spies from around the world on how to fight and survive if they found themselves in danger behind enemy lines.

Major William D. Frazer

In 1929, William D Frazer wrote a book called American Pistol Shooting. The formalized idea of shooting with vision on the target, not on the sights, now had an American authors seal of approval. Frazer was not an all-or-nothing advocate for sights or no sights; he thought each technique had its place. Frazer's breakdown was not new, and many of the same principles that Fairbairn had conceptualized were evident. Frazer believed that defensive shooting would involve pistols at close range, aimed at large targets by pointing the gun and shooting rapidly.

Capt. Charles Askins, Jr

In 1939, Captain Askins (later Col. Askins) wrote The Art of Handgun Shooting. It was a soup-to-nuts guide for handgunners. Whether an information-seeking novice or an established aficionado, Askins had something for everyone. He dedicated chapter 21 to what he termed Shooting by Instinctive Pointing. Early in the text, he said:

I'd be willing to gamble that I could take a group of rookie officers and by teaching them shooting by pointing - and not by elaborate aiming -could make them just as expert in practical defensive shooting as by the usual methods of sight alignment.

I agree with his theory. Moreover, I have done it. I have trained thousands of law enforcement professionals to use TFS as their first aiming tool. They achieved levels of speed and accuracy that were beyond their expectations.

Askins did not believe in shooting from the hip - he considered that level of accuracy to be unreliable. Askins was a proponent of single-handed shooting with the gun out from the body about 12-14 inches and in line with his wishbone. Askins considered training at 30-36 feet a practical maximum distance. Beyond that, he found that accuracy was less effective. Once back to 50 feet, Askins could only score hits with about 80% reliability out on a human-sized target. Beyond that, he advocated for the use of sights.

Col. Rex Applegate

In 1940, Fairbairn met Rex Applegate in quite a dramatic style - Fairbairn was doing a demonstration of hand-to-hand combat for a U.S intelligence agency called the Office of Strategic Services (OSS), and a cocky, younger, bigger, heavier Applegate was his chosen stooge. Fairbairn was 57 years old, 5'10, and 160 lbs. in weight. Fairbairn demanded Applegate attack him full force, for real. Applegate did, and a moment later, when he found himself in a crumpled heap on the floor, he decided this old guy could teach him a thing or two. In 1943, Applegate wrote a classic text on close combat titled Kill or Get Killed.

Applegate took Fairbairn's approach to point shooting and ran with it. He classified it as "instinctive pointing". He adjusted the technique to progress from the low gun (around waist height) to the high and up in front of the face. Aside from that, the principles were the same; still focusing on speed, due to a lack of distance or time, and instinctive aim instead of sight use. Applegate believed it was *the* technique and advocated its use for distances of 50 feet. Applegate still considered the ability to use sights a relevant part of training. He did not believe sights were the appropriate aiming system unless there was time or distance between the shooter and his opponent. Applegate also collaborated with Michael D. Janich, writing a textbook on point shooting called Bullseyes Don't Shoot Back, published in 1998.

William H. "Bill" Jordan

In 1965, William H. "Bill" Jordan wrote a book named No Second Place Winner. At the time of writing, Bill was a 30-year border patrol veteran and held the rank of Assistant Chief Patrol Inspector. Bill was famous for being a fast and accurate shooter. He spoke from a position as a practitioner and as a trainer. Bill believed there was a time and place for deliberate aim of the pistol held up in front of the eyes with intent to use the sights. Bill also believed there was a time when such an approach would lead to your demise since it took too long, hence the second-place reference. His book title is slightly more subtle than Applegate's Kill or be Killed, but his message is similar. Speed is crucial when you are close to someone who needs to be shot. There is no time for extraneous movement, style consideration, or sight use. Bill broke his technique selection down to yardage.

- He defined 0 to 3 yards as "point blank." He recommended drawing the pistol from the holster and rocking it into alignment with the target as soon as it clears. This is a one-handed technique, holding the pistol at about waist height. Bill described it as "very fast"

- The next range he accounted for was 3 - 7 yards. At this distance, the pistol draw progressed more. It is still done with just one hand, but it is forward of the torso and higher than the waistline. He described the stopping point as when the shoulder muscles stop the arm

21

- 7 - 15 yards was similar in gun position relative to the body, but Bill now advocated adding the second hand. He particularly advised this if multiple shots were necessary. The gun was still occupying the lower half of the torso. Above belt height, but lower than the sternum

- 15 - 25 yards (and beyond). These distances required sights, and the advised pistol position was a two-handed grip. The arms were extended, and the gun was at eye level, and Bill's stance selection was very isosceles

Bill referenced a phrase in his book that was common sixty years ago, but even then, its origin was unknown: "Speed is fine, but accuracy is final." He added his caveat to that: "If you are given the time to display it."

William S. Cassidy

William L. Cassidy wrote the most comprehensive work on the history of target-focused shooting in 1978. The book was entitled Quick or Dead. The author did a fantastic job of researching and thoroughly referencing the sources. Quick or Dead is a worthy read, and I highly recommend it.

Regarding technique, Cassidy writes very thoroughly on his preferred methodology. He explains how and why with illustrations to complement the written detail. Cassidy approves hip shooting at distances of 9 feet or less. Any further than that, and he did not consider accuracy to be reliably achievable.

From 9 to 25 feet, Cassidy prefers the gun to be brought up to eye level, still using a single hand to shoot, still looking at the intended target. Beyond 25 feet, Cassidy encourages a two-handed grip and the use of sights.

Chuck Klein

In 1986, Chuck Klein released his first edition of Instinct Combat Shooting. Three updated editions were published over the following three decades. The title has been in continuous print since it was first published. Klein had an interesting and diverse career; he served as a law enforcement officer but was also a writer, editor, and firearms instructor. Like many other proponents of the concept, Klein endorsed two eyes open, intense visual attention on the intended target, and disregard for sights on the handgun in close-quarters engagements. Klein limited the effective distance of the technique to within 10 yards. His term for the technique is captured in the title of his book. He defines Instinct Combat Shooting as:

The act of operating a HANDGUN by focusing on the target, as opposed to the sights, and instinctively coordinating the hand and mind to cause the HANDGUN to discharge at a time and point that ensures interception of the projectile with the target.

Ralph Mroz

In 2000, Ralph Mroz published Defensive Shooting for Real-Life Encounters. He dedicates a chapter to point shooting and references the concept throughout. Mroz was open to many things and had no ego-driven absolutism about technique. Mroz asked all the right questions and did not pretend to have all the answers. He drew on industry expertise and scientific research for his work. A quarter of a century later, there have been some advances in research and physiology, but many of his big questions remain a mystery. Mroz defined the difference between sighted and point shooting as follows:

Sighted shooting is best defined as using an object in between your eyes and the target to align the gun with the target. Usually, one or both sights are so used, but the silhouette of the gun itself may be used, as may some other features of the gun. Point shooting is best understood as relying on your 'pointing' ability to index the gun to the target. It may be done from the hip, chest height, at eye level, or anywhere at all.

Mroz considered Applegate's technique the standard against which to assess point shooting. He was vehemently against hip-shooting as a valid technique. He believed hip shooting had long been discredited as a valuable field skill. He added a caveat to his dismissal: if someone was as talented and willing to practice as much as Bill Jordan, they could feel free to hip-shoot!

Lou Chiodo

Lou Chiodo is a retired law enforcement veteran who brought together an extraordinary combination of military, martial arts, and police experience. A former Captain in the United States Marine Corps, he served with distinction before transitioning to civilian law enforcement. As a patrol officer in California with decades of experience, Chiodo witnessed firsthand the disconnect between traditional firearms training and the realities of armed confrontations.

Chiodo recognized a fundamental problem plaguing law enforcement firearms training. Slow and steady marksmanship courses with small groups and lots of time were not a reality. The qualification scores satisfied administrative requirements but bore little resemblance to what officers encountered in actual close, fast, armed confrontations.

Chiodo harnessed the proven methods of legendary instructors William Fairbairn, Rex Applegate, Ralph Mroz, and Robert Taubert. Central to his philosophy was the belief that practical law enforcement training must simulate real-world conditions. Training should be evidence-informed, focusing on proximity, speed, and officers' training to be target-focused, not gun-focused. In 2009, Chiodo published his book, Winning a High-Speed, Close-Distance

Gunfight. The book captured his core philosophy, exemplified in my favorite of his quotes:

The purpose of firearms training is to prepare an individual to use firearms in a fight against an adversary in what usually begins as a spontaneous attack initiated by the adversary. Our firearms program is not about shooting. It is about fighting. When the concept of fighting is taken out of firearms training, we have forgotten the purpose of our training.

Chiodo challenged conventional wisdom by addressing the complete spectrum of armed encounters—from the psychological and physiological effects of survival stress to the need for officers to respond decisively and effectively.

Robert K. "Bob" Taubert

In 2012, Bob Taubert, a United States Marine Corps combat veteran and FBI retiree, wrote Rattenkrieg! The Art and Science of Close-Quarter Battle. The book focused on pistol techniques in close quarters. Taubert believed that close-quarter battle skills needed to be separated from unrealistic range training protocols.

Much of Taubert's work related to preplanned operations and training for hostage rescue; for this work, he demanded precise or surgical shots with a sighting system. Taubert also believed that it was appropriate to aim within a maximum of 30 feet using a "Target Focused" technique. The circumstances for employing this adaptive aiming process require the target to be close or wide open (no hostage in the way). Even when remaining 100% target-focused, Taubert still required the pistol to be raised to eye level. The only exception to that eye-level height was when time or space prevented it; in that circumstance, he considered hip shooting an option.

Conclusion

As each of these authors seems to repeat, the distance you find yourself from the target, the size of that target, and the content of the terrain surrounding the target dictate how aiming should take place. A modern handgun can be accurate at 1 yard, 10 yards, or, in the right hands, even 100 yards. The proximity of the target, the available time, and the size of the target will determine the most expeditious technique for aiming the gun.

Over one hundred years ago, this technique was the relevant benchmark for training officers to prevail in close-quarter exchanges of violence/gunfire. One hundred years later, this training has fallen by the wayside, and the problem of officers being shot and killed while extremely close to their attackers remains the same.

For those who say the technique has no place, have never tried it, or have never considered teaching it, I challenge you to read on.

CHAPTER 3 - IT IS ALL AIMING

You always hit what you're aiming at. You aren't always aiming at what you want to hit.

- Leon Reha

The question isn't whether you aimed—it's whether you aimed where you intended. There is no such thing as unaimed fire. Reckless or negligent shots are not acceptable. Aiming must be intentional. There is no spray-and-pray approach that can be deemed credible or legitimate. There may be sighted or unsighted fire - but it is ALL AIMED. The very definition of the word aim has nothing to do with sights. Here are some dictionary quotes to confirm this potential revelation:

Meriam Webster: Aim – to point a weapon at an object

Cambridge: Aim – the act of pointing a weapon toward something

Dictionary.com: Aim - to position or direct (a firearm, ball, arrow, rocket, etc.) so that, on firing or release, the discharged projectile will hit a target or travel along a certain path

The paradox of always hitting what you're aiming at lies at the heart of understanding how to achieve accuracy. The bullet doesn't lie. It travels exactly where the muzzle was pointed when the trigger was pressed. If your shot missed your intended target, (equipment failure aside) you didn't miss because the bullet went astray—you missed because you aimed somewhere other than where you thought you were aiming.

Understanding this distinction is critical. Most shooters who miss their target believe they executed correctly but were betrayed by their equipment, the conditions, or simple bad luck. The uncomfortable truth is more instructive: the gun performed exactly as designed. The bullet followed its predetermined, predictable path with precision. What failed was the alignment between intention and execution, between where the shooter believed they were aiming and where the muzzle pointed.

This realization is liberating rather than discouraging. If the problem isn't the equipment (a rare exception) or chance, then the solution lies entirely within the shooter's control. Mechanics can be trained, the process can be refined, and the gap between intention and consistent reality can be closed.

The Fundamental Truth About Aiming and Accuracy

Accurately shooting a gun involves just two things. It is simple, but not easy.

1. Point the muzzle at what you want to hit

2. Move the trigger without moving the muzzle

These two elements sound almost trivially straightforward when written out this way. Yet the challenge lies in their seamless integration. The first without the second is mere preparation. The second, without maintaining the first, is sabotage. Both must occur simultaneously, in perfect harmony, for the shot to land where intended.

Consider what happens in the moment of the trigger press. The shooter has aligned the muzzle, acquired the target, and perhaps even confirmed the alignment with sights. Everything appears ready. Then the trigger begins its rearward travel. This seemingly simple mechanical action introduces force into a carefully balanced system. Muscles tense. The hand adjusts its grip imperceptibly. The muzzle shifts—perhaps only fractions of an inch, perhaps only for fractions of a second. The trigger press is the final act of aiming – it is usually the reason for not hitting what was intended. Any disruption of muzzle alignment during the trigger press redirects the weapon, creating a disconnect between the intended action and the actual outcome.

Most shooters dedicate substantial time to confirming the first element—pointing the muzzle correctly. They practice sight alignment, sight picture in search of the illusion of perfection. But the second element—moving the trigger without disturbing that carefully established aim—receives far less attention despite being the more common point of failure. It's the moment where good preparation either culminates in success or unravels into disappointment.

Every trigger press is a moment of truth—in that moment, when the primer is struck, all preparation, all training, all intention converges into a single, irreversible act. The firearm points where it points. The bullet goes where it goes. And you discover what you were truly aiming at. Without understanding how to sustain aim while moving the trigger, sighting systems are a waste of time.

This moment cannot be recalled or revised. There is no opportunity for adjustment once the primer is struck. The shot exists in objective reality, immune to explanation or justification. A shooter's internal narrative about what was intended becomes irrelevant. Only the outcome matters.

This truth is why the target is such a profound teacher in training. It strips away pretense and reveals truth with uncompromising clarity. There is no arguing with physics. There is no negotiating with ballistics. There is only the honest accounting of where you aimed and where you hit.

The target provides feedback that is both immediate and absolute. It doesn't care about experience level, excuses, or self-perception. The target simply shows the result of the shooter's actions. This brutal honesty makes the target the most valuable and honest training partner you will ever have. Every hole in training tells a story—not the story you might want to tell yourself, but the story of what happened when metal met paper.

When shooters learn to accept this feedback without defensiveness, when the target in training is considered a teacher rather than a judge, improvement becomes inevitable. You learn to feel the difference between a trigger press that maintains aim and one that disrupts it. Shooters transform from someone who hopes to hit the target, to someone who knows how to make it happen.

CHAPTER 4 - THE TRAINING AND

REALITY GAP

Handgun qualification for the police, something originally conceived as a test of marksmanship proficiency for soldiers and competitive shooters, still consists of shooting at fixed numbers of clearly defined targets at well-known distances, standard firing elements and sequences, liberal time limits, and arbitrary threshold scores. The rote firing of time-honoured courses and their derivatives produces well-practised range marksmen, but it does not assess their ability to perform in gunfights.

- Morrison, 1998

The qualification-based approach to firearms training is failing our law enforcement officers, armed professionals, and the communities they serve. Somehow, deluded training practices have us believing that to become a gunfighter, we only have to check a box by passing the firearms qualification. Nothing could be further from the truth.

Current training predominantly encourages shooting under controlled conditions on stationary targets, in good lighting with clear backstops and abundant time. Shooters meticulously align sights, control breathing, and execute slow trigger movements without making a single tactical decision. Success is measured by achieving passing scores and tight shot groups. This methodology is a foundational factor in why our people do not develop transferable skills that function beyond a target shooting environment.

Those brave badge wearers who take an oath to protect us do not have the luxury of time in the critical moments of a close-quarter engagement. They are unlikely to be standing stationary, carefully aligning sights, or focusing on achieving tight shot groups in perfect lighting conditions. However, traditional firearms practice and testing continue to emphasize these elements exclusively, creating a dangerous disconnect between training and reality. The disconnect seems to be well known; it has been written about in the context of police training for decades (Roberts & Bristow, 1969).

When people experience life-or-death encounters after traditional firearms training, they are compelled to perform at speeds they have never practiced. Their brains attempt to deploy skills at survival speed. They try to operate their guns at the pace they need, not the pace they have practiced. This often results in poor performance and low accuracy (Donner & Popovich, 2019). They are attempting to do something they have never rehearsed; they are creating a new solution to a problem they have never faced, all while experiencing the most terrifying moments of their lives. The middle of a gunfight is a terrible time to learn a new skill.

This speed-and-context disconnect becomes starkly apparent when reviewing video footage of an officer-involved shooting. Examine the environment where the incident occurred. Is there anything visually similar to the range training setup? Then, close your eyes and listen to the speed of fire. Does your organization regularly train to achieve that level of speed while maintaining the accuracy required for the life-saving objective? In addition to relevant speed and surroundings, we also need to consider whether the range aids in decision-making preparation.

Vision and attention are limited resources. Together, they facilitate high-quality decision-making in critical situations. Practicing where to direct these limited resources is essential for making the best possible decisions. The information that influences use-of-force decisions comes from external sources. Training must focus on directing vision and attention outward. During live fire training, instructors should consider the following:

- Psychological and physiological reasons for remaining target-focused in close-quarters situations
- Evidence-informed insights into required response speeds
- Techniques for building confidence in target-focused shooting
- Research-backed data demonstrating the need for movement and urgency in close quarters

Fundamental skills begin at the live-fire range, but training does not end there. The range is just one component in developing robust, transferable skills that seamlessly transition to high-fidelity training and operational application. Underlying principles of training should include:

- Speed and accuracy standards aligned with operational objectives
- Preparing officers for the reality of close-quarters engagements
- Enhancing decision-making under stress
- Practical application beyond the firing line

Training must not be solely focused on qualifications. Training for test-taking is not a valuable investment of time and resources. To categorize test preparation as relevant real-world training is a fallacy. Exclusively devoting time to the test and nothing else is negligent, and not just in the civil sense of the word. Instead, training must be intentionally focused on operationally relevant skills, ensuring that people are genuinely prepared for the challenges they may face, not just the tests they must pass.

This disparity between misguided training and the demands of reality is not new. Fifty years ago, Col. Rex Applegate wrote about Military training that didn't go beyond simple target shooting. The same comparable flaws in transferable skills still exist today.

Early in World War II, it was found that target shooting skill with the handgun was not enough for the soldier in combat. It was proved that a man trained only in the target phase of the handgun was proficient up to the point where he could kill an enemy only when he had time to aim and fire, and providing he could see the sights. Unfortunately, such ideal conditions were found to be the exception in most close combat situations.

- Applegate, 1976

CHAPTER 5 - AN EVIDENCE-INFORMED APPROACH

Neither doctrinal, technical, nor tactical developments were driven by research or programme evaluation, but, rather, by trainers' various notions about good sense as constrained by resources.

- Morrison, 1998

The firearms training curriculum for law enforcement is typically not driven by evidence. It is driven by dogma and tradition. Trainers routinely build programs around a qualification standard—I use the word standard loosely. The idea that meeting a mark designed to be achievable by every person, including the lowest common denominator, sets the bar so low that it is barely a bar.

Traditional law enforcement firearms training, which focuses primarily on static target practice and basic marksmanship, fails to prepare officers adequately for the dynamic nature of real-world encounters.

The war cry of armies of instructors is to focus unwaveringly on the front sight. This strategy has become the standard after decades of target shooting schools, which have defined what most people know and experience. This strategy of meticulous, irrelevantly timed aiming works well when the target is predetermined and clearly defined, such as one hanging on a range. However, it is a conflicting suggestion when the deciding factor about when and if to shoot is information from human behavior, which is going to be sourced beyond the gun's sighting system.

Simply put, looking at what you might have to shoot allows for better decision-making. When a handgun obstructs the user's vision, we make less reliable decisions (Taylor, 2021). The longer we look at our subject, the more information we gather, and the better our decisions are (Vickers & Lewinski, 2012). When speed matters, sights are a disadvantage (Lewinski et al., 2015).

Do not misconstrue the suggestion of looking at the subject longer as guidance to delay an appropriately timed response to a stimulus. If people need to be shot, shoot them until they do not need to be shot anymore.

By looking at the subject longer rather than at our gun, we have the opportunity to gather more information. In the final fractions of a second, when lives are at risk and about to be changed forever, pertinent information allows for a better decision. Things can happen and change in the blink of an eye – or sometimes even quicker than that!

A growing body of research supports the importance of knowing where to look. The following studies focus on U.S. law enforcement handgun skills, and the high-level overview focuses on the inferences relevant to TFS in close quarters. Although they are law enforcement-based studies, the elements of human performance apply to armed professionals in general.

Please take the time to read the original papers in their entirety. There is a wealth of knowledge and guidance to be harvested.

Engineering Resilience Into Split-Second Shoot/No Shoot Decisions: The Effect of Muzzle-Position

The objective of resilience engineering is to reduce the complexity of the work place – the true enemy of consistently achieving desired results (e.g., Dekker, 2001, 2014; Woods et al., 2010) – and thereby improve the likelihood for success and safety rather than errors and accidents.

- Taylor, 2021

Dr Paul Taylor completed this study in 2021. His primary question was about the relevance of the preparatory handgun position and its impact on officers' ability to make high-quality decisions, intertwined with how that position may affect response times.

Although this was not a primarily TFS-oriented study on aiming the pistol, it provides insight into the advantage of remaining target-focused for as long as possible when using a pistol. For that reason, I have included it here; it provides a holistic view of how prolonged vision and attention focused outward can benefit the officer working under time constraints.

Taylor conducted a randomized controlled experiment. His participants were more than 300 active law enforcement officers from more than 20 agencies. He used a firearms simulator to achieve consistency in the scenarios he presented to each officer. The officers were randomly assigned to use one of three muzzle positions and told to maintain that position unless they decided to shoot. The positions used were described as:

- Aiming: The sights of the gun were held in alignment with the officer's visual gaze, pointed at the projector screen and the index finger was to be off the trigger and resting along the slide of the training pistol

- High Ready Position: The gun was held at the level of the officer's sternum, and the index finger was to be off the trigger and resting along the slide of the training pistol

- Low Ready Position: The gun was held at the level of the officer's navel, and the index finger was to be off the trigger and resting along the slide of the training pistol

The videos the officers were randomly assigned to had two potential scenario options. Sometimes the subject in the video presented a gun, sometimes the subject presented a cell phone. The results showed a measurable difference in the accuracy of decisions based on gun position.

One hundred and thirty-nine of the officers were presented with the 'shoot' scenario; they all fired their handguns toward the subject. One hundred seventy-four officers were presented with the cell phone or 'no shoot' scenario. Eighty-nine of those officers fired their handguns. Of those eighty-nine who made the decision error, only 18% were starting from the low-ready position. The other 82% started from the high ready and the aiming position. Even though there was a massive disparity in the decision quality, the response time was relatively less divergent. The average difference across all the positions was a mere 11/100ths of a second.

In contrast to the minimal difference in time between these positions, the difference in the decision-making process was substantial. The officers who started at the aimed position were more than twice as likely to make a shooting error. That is, the officers who had the gun prioritized in their field of view were twice as likely to shoot a person who produced a cell phone.

Taylor's research demonstrates that an officer's ability to maintain clear visual contact with subjects may be more critical than traditionally assumed. The study found that officers who maintained unobstructed observation of the subjects made significantly fewer shooting errors compared to those who aimed directly at subjects or had the pistol in a high ready position. The research revealed that officers' arms, hands, and firearms can obstruct crucial visual information. This obstruction forces officers to interpret potential threats based on limited visible movement, potentially leading to misinterpretation and unnecessary use of force.

Maintaining clear visual contact with subjects, including the ability to observe facial expressions, body language, and the full range of movement, may be more valuable than traditional weapon training. This approach enhances threat assessment accuracy and communication opportunities, potentially reducing the likelihood of unnecessary force while maintaining officer safety.

Dr. Taylor's study provides compelling evidence that law enforcement training should emphasize unobstructed subject observation as a key component of threat assessment and force decision-making protocols.

The Real Risks During Deadly Police Shootouts

The results of this study indicate that officers had no advantage over intermediate shooters and a small advantage over novices.

- Lewinski et al., 2015

Dr. Lewinski's 2015 study was a novel approach to research regarding law enforcement gunfight data. Though the research in this realm is somewhat limited, the studies that have been conducted focus on the officers' skills and performance. Little formal research examines the abilities of the subjects who attack the officers. Dr. Lewinski strove to examine how effective people could be using a handgun, especially if they have little or no training.

Dr. Lewinski used two hundred and forty-seven subjects for his study. He classified them based on their training and experience with using a handgun. He put them into three broad categories:

- Expert: These test subjects had completed formal law enforcement firearms training and/or military training in handgun use. There were eighty-three people in this group

- Intermediate: This group had no formal law enforcement training but had recreationally shot handguns or rifles in the past. This category also included subjects with military training primarily focused on using rifles and carbines. There were seventy-one people in this group

- Novice: These subjects had absolutely no experience or training in firearms. This group also contained people who had fired a weapon, perhaps once or twice, before. There were ninety-three people in this group

The subjects were told to shoot nine targets, each from a different distance. Three rounds were fired at each target as quickly as possible without compromising accuracy. They were not told where on the target to aim. The distances were completed in a random sequence.

- Between 3 and 15 feet, they fired 9 rounds
- Between 18 and 45 feet, they fired 12 rounds
- Between 60 and 75 feet, they fired 6 rounds

The novice shooters achieved 75% accuracy between 3 and 15 feet. The intermediate and expert shooters were only marginally more accurate, scoring 84% and 88%, respectively. Dr. Lewinski found these accuracy results "unexpected" and "alarming." Dr. Lewinski references data in his research that suggests that almost half of all law enforcement shootings occur within this distance, and officers need a greater advantage than they currently have.

Another fascinating study area was the novices and their decisions regarding their point of aim. None of the participants were instructed to aim at any part of the target, a silhouette shape of a human torso and head. As expected, most of the trained participants, the experts, aimed for the center of the upper thoracic cavity, as their training would have encouraged them to do so. Most of the novices, lacking any formal training, chose to aim at the head when they were 3 feet from the target. As the distance increased, the novices adjusted their point of aim and shifted to the larger target area, the torso.

The research reveals a troubling gap between training outcomes and real-world requirements. Dr. Lewinski argues that law enforcement agencies must fundamentally restructure their firearms and tactical training approach. They must move beyond traditional marksmanship to develop comprehensive programs that better prepare officers for the realities of close-quarter encounters.

The research indicates that current training programs may need substantial revision to better prepare officers for close-quarters combat, where speed and accuracy are equally vital for survival. Dr. Lewinski suggests that departments implement more frequent, varied, realistic training scenarios integrating movement, decision-making, and shooting skills. He also advocated that training should be designed to develop expertise that keeps cognition and vision externally focused on the subject and the dynamic event in which the officer is involved.

Ambushes Leading Cause of Officer Fatalities When Every Second Counts: Analysis of Officer Movement from Trained Ready Tactical Positions

Not surprisingly, officers using point or instinct shooting were significantly faster in firing from each position (p < 0.01 for all positions).

- Lewinski et al., 2015

This 2015 study was primarily focused on measuring the speed of officer response. The research was based on two experiments. The first question being considered was the placement of the trigger finger prior to shooting and its impact on speed of response. The second experiment focused on ready positions and shooting positions, again assessing the speed of the response achieved by the officer. The researchers were seeking data to be able to ascertain if there was an advantageous position that would allow a faster response by officers who were faced with an unprovoked surprise attack.

The first study assessed trigger finger placement. Fifty-two law enforcement officers volunteered to participate in the study. Four different trigger finger positions were tested. The researchers described them as:

- Straight ahead on trigger guard
- Straight ahead on trigger guard but with a c-curve

- At a slight 15° angle on the frame
- At about a 30° angle placed on the slide

The original study has accompanying images for those interested in more specific details regarding the trigger finger position. Each participant fired three times from each of the four start positions, for a total of twelve rounds. The participants completed the task in their own time, that is they were not given a start signal for each iteration. They began when they were ready. The researcher used high-speed video to record movement. They subsequently analyzed movement time; there was no reaction time measured for these movements. The participants were told to fire as quickly as possible and to shoot without aiming (I would respectfully suggest this would have been better described as unsighted).

Some of the participants disregarded this instruction, moved cautiously, and took the time to use sights. The researchers put this down to habit. Subsequently, the researchers divided the participants into two groups: no aim and aim. The results regarding the speed of firing the gun were unsurprising; the groups that used sights were significantly slower than the group that pointed. That difference in discharge time was an average of 0.35 seconds.

Another interesting variable that separated the sight users was how long it took them to contact the trigger. The officers who decided to use sights were measurably slower in moving their trigger finger from the start position to contacting the trigger. The average time to move to touch the trigger was doubled for those who aimed using sights, from 0.11 seconds to 0.22 seconds.

The second study was focused on ready positions. Sixty-eight law enforcement officers volunteered to participate in the study. There were twenty different potential tasks to complete. Each officer was randomly assigned to ten of those twenty tasks. Three of the tasks were completed using a shotgun. The other seventeen were handgun ready positions and shooting positions. The handgun positions were:

- Weapon on Target, Indexed Finger
- Weapon on Target, Finger on Trigger
- Weapon on Target, Indexed Finger, 3 Round Burst
- Weapon on Target, Finger on Trigger, 3 Round Burst
- Weapon in Holster, Snapped
- Weapon in Holster, Unsnapped
- Weapon in Holster into Combat Tuck
- Low-Ready, Indexed Finger, Aim
- Low-Ready, Indexed Finger, Point
- High Ready, Aim
- Close Ready, Aim

- Close Ready, Point

- Belt Tuck, Aim

- Weapon in High-Guard, Aim

- Weapon in High-Guard, Point

- Weapon in Bootleg (held behind thigh), Aim

- Weapon in Bootleg, Combat Tuck

The original study includes images to accompany the positions, providing clarification for those interested in understanding what was tested. As shown in the breakdown of positions, some tasks were instructed to be completed using sights, while others were to be completed by pointing. The participants were timed using a shot timer as a stimulus. On the audible cue of the timer, they completed their assigned tasks. The time recorded would also be inclusive of the reaction time to that audible cue.

A critical finding in this research is the life-or-death importance of response speed in law enforcement encounters, particularly regarding the disparity between point shooting and sighted fire in close-quarter situations. The study reveals compelling evidence that could significantly impact officer survival and training protocols. When referring to 'aimed fire' in this study, the sight use was minimal; the participants were not expected to seek perfect alignment, just to get a glimpse and fire as rapidly as possible. It seems that even a simple shift of vision and attention in a low-stress, no-decision environment, just for a glimpse of their sight, costs them all precious time.

The research demonstrates that point shooting consistently proves faster than sight use across all firing positions, with officers saving more than 0.30 seconds when using point shooting techniques. This seemingly small-time difference becomes particularly crucial when considering that suspects can draw and fire a weapon in as little as 0.23 seconds, with an average time of 0.53 seconds (Lewinski et al., 2013). Officers already face an inherent time disadvantage due to the necessary threat recognition and decision-making process, which takes between 0.46 and 0.70 seconds (Lewinski et al., 2014). Therefore, any additional delay in response time could prove fatal in a close-quarter encounter.

When examining specific ready positions, the Low-Ready position emerged as the fastest overall, with officers able to point shoot in 0.64 seconds compared to 0.97 seconds when using sighted fire. Similar patterns emerged from other positions, with Close-Ready showing point shooting times of 0.74 seconds versus 1.03 seconds for sighted fire and High-Guard demonstrating 0.73 seconds for point shooting compared to 1.13 seconds when using sights (Lewinski et al., 2015). These consistent findings across different positions underscore the significant time advantage that unsighted aiming provides.

The implications for close-quarter combat are particularly relevant. In proximity, taking unnecessary time to acquire and align sights could create a dangerous delay in response time. Previous research supports this finding, showing that officers who use point-shooting techniques by driving their weapon through their line of gaze rather than focusing on sight alignment demonstrate increased speed and accuracy at intermediate distances (Vickers & Lewinski, 2012).

This research suggests that law enforcement training programs should incorporate regular point-shooting practices, particularly for close-quarter situations where rapid response times are crucial for survival. Given the speed at which confrontations unfold, particularly in ambush situations, officers need every possible advantage concerning response time. The data suggests that the traditional emphasis on sight alignment might need to be reconsidered in favor of point shooting techniques in close-quarter situations, provided officers receive adequate training to maintain accuracy at these shorter distances.

This research provides valuable insights for law enforcement training programs. It suggests balancing traditional marksmanship training with practical close-quarter techniques, emphasizing speed while maintaining acceptable accuracy. The findings indicate that target-focused shooting should be considered a crucial skill for officers, particularly in situations where rapid response times could mean the difference between life and death.

Performing Under Pressure: Gaze Control, Decision-Making, and Shooting Performance of Elite and Rookie Police Officers.

If these changes in firearm's training were implemented then the gaze control of novice officers should be similar to that of elite athletes and elite officers from the first day of training, thereby increasing the likelihood that they would be able to maintain visual control over any situation they encountered.

- Vickers & Lewinski, 2012

This groundbreaking study by Vickers and Lewinski in 2012 provides compelling empirical evidence that may answer some questions about the relevance of target-focused vision and attention in close-range defensive encounters. Their research compared rookie and elite police officer performance during simulated lethal force encounters. They found differences in how the officers directed their vision, made decisions, and in their shooting performance. The results revealed striking differences in how top performers approach the targeting task compared to novices.

Twenty-four officers volunteered to participate in this study. Eleven of the officers were termed to be elite; they were members of an Emergency Response Team. The other thirteen participants were from the same department at the end of their initial training and were termed rookies. The scenario they encountered lasted for approximately one minute. They were observing a male subject becoming agitated with a polite but unhelpful receptionist. The culmination of the subject's frustration led to him pivoting and presenting either a cell phone or a handgun toward the officers. Each officer was wearing eye-tracking equipment, and the data captured included where their gaze was fixated throughout the incident, as well as the accuracy of their shooting, if they decided to shoot the subject.

Gaze Control Differences:

- Elite officers maintained their gaze on the threat/target rather than their weapon sights, with 71% of their final fixations on the assailant's weapon or cell phone (increasing to 86% during successful hits)

- Rookies, likely following traditional firearms training, attempted to look at their weapon sights 39% of the time in their final fixations. They jerked their gaze abruptly to their weapon on 84% of trials

Where the officers looked significantly influenced their speed, accuracy, and decision-making. Elite officers achieved high-performance criteria (accurate shots, firing before the assailant, proper decision-making) in 75% of trials, while rookie officers only met these criteria in 52.86% of trials. The elite officers hit their target 74.54% of the time, compared to 53.85% for rookies. They also fired before the assailant 92.50% of the time, compared to 42.22% for rookies. Regarding decision-making, only 18.18% of elite officers fired when a cell phone was drawn, whereas 61.54% of rookie officers incorrectly fired when seeing a cell phone.

This study provides empirical support for the importance of where vision and attention are focused in close-range, high-stress encounters with limited time. The elite performers prioritized a target-focused approach rather than a sight-focused one. They also knew where to look on the target for pertinent information, versus the sporadic gaze patterns exhibited by the rookies. The authors note that this allocation of visual resources aligns with previous research on elite athletes in pistol, rifle, and shotgun sports, where top performers maintained target focus and brought the gun to their line of sight rather than switching between the target and their weapon sights (Ripoll et al., 1985).

The researchers emphasize that the type of training a person initially receives often dictates how well they perform in the future. This is a crucial insight because it suggests that early training methods can create lasting patterns in performance. They argue that current firearms training inadvertently creates a problematic sequence where officers learn to focus first on their weapon sights. Instead, they recommend reversing this sequence in initial training by first establishing the line of gaze on the target.

The researchers suggest that this change in the initial training approach would improve novice officers' decision-making, shooting performance, and gaze control patterns, aligning them more closely with those of elite officers. This recommendation is particularly significant because it challenges traditional firearms training methods emphasizing sight focus. The researchers argue that changing this foundational training approach could help officers maintain better visual control in real-world situations, potentially reducing errors in decision-making and shooting accuracy.

This also connects to their broader findings about how difficult it is to change ingrained training patterns. In their study, the rookies reverted to using their sights under stress, resulting in a problematic saccade (rapid eye movement between fixation points - see vision chapter) to their weapon 84% of the time, which disrupted their ability to maintain awareness of the threat.

Kinematic Analysis of Naive Shooters in Common Law Enforcement Encounters

When officers are faced with a threat from an assailant, it takes approximately 0.46 to 0.70 seconds to recognize and process the threat and to begin a physical response, and up to 1.94 seconds to un-holster their firearm and return fire.

- Kantor et al., 2022

This 2022 study shared a similar focus to Dr. Lewinski's 2015 research on the accuracy of naïve shooters (Lewinski et al., 2015), in that the researchers examined the ability of naïve shooters, rather than the officers. This research offered some alarming data regarding the speed at which an attack could occur.

The researchers determined the most common demographics of people involved in shooting at police officers. They recruited their volunteers based on those parameters. They selected twenty males between the ages of 18 and 37 years. None of the males reported ever having had prior firearms training. Eight different scenarios were identified for the study based on prior research. Three were stationary scenarios, and five involved the subject shooting and then fleeing. Each of the scenarios required the male subject to fire at a target resembling a police officer. The scenarios were as follows:

- Assailant seated in the driver's seat with a gun in their hand and simulating shooting out of a driver's side window
- Assailant, seated in the driver's seat, with a gun in their hand and shooting out of the passenger's side window
- Assailant facing a target resembling an LEO and drawing a pistol from their waistband, pointing, and shooting
- 90° Turn: Assailant with the weapon held in their hand and concealed on their posterior thigh, focused on the face of the officer. The weapon was rapidly pointed and fired, followed by a 90° angle turn and flight
- 180° Turn: Assailant facing the target with the weapon held in their hand in the bootleg position, rapidly points and fires at the target followed by a 180° turn and flight away from the target
- Strong Side Turn: Assailant has their back facing the target with the weapon held in their hand and concealed on the anterior thigh, turns rapidly to shoot and then flee
- Assailant while fleeing moves the gun cross body, and under the opposite arm, points it back toward the officer and shoots
- Assailant fleeing the officer and pointing the gun and shooting over the opposite shoulder

The subjects were shown a slow-motion video of each task they were assigned to complete, and then a full-speed video. They were allowed two to three practice attempts to make sure they understood the task. The researchers deemed this sufficient for safety, but not enough repetitions to allow for any motor learning effects. Each subject then completed three recorded time trials. They were not given a cue to begin, so there was no reaction time to account for. They moved when they wanted to, and the measurement began when their movement began. This lends itself to the reality of an officer's observations. The first clue to the subject initiating the attack was movement. There was no falsification of perception, as no audible or visual clue was used to add reaction time.

The results demonstrated that untrained individuals could draw and fire weapons with surprising speed, often faster than trained officers could respond. The research shows naive shooters could draw and fire in as little as 0.81 seconds, depending on the scenario, with vehicle-based shootings occurring as fast as 0.28 seconds. More concerning, when turning and shooting while fleeing, subjects could complete the action in an average time of 0.38-0.49 seconds, with their backs fully turned within 0.4 seconds after firing.

For comparison, studies indicate officers typically need 0.37 seconds to recognize and begin reacting to a threat, with up to 2.17 seconds total required to identify a threat and return fire (Lewinski & Dysterheft, 2015). Even with weapons already drawn and aimed, officers need 0.25 seconds to pull the trigger, which extends to 0.56 seconds when making shoot/do not shoot decisions (Lewinski et al., 2014).

The situation becomes even more complex when an officer is already under fire. Blair et al. (2016) found that most officer deaths from gunfire occurred within the first few seconds of engagement, highlighting the critical nature of these initial moments. Research shows that when already under fire, officer response times can be further impacted by up to 20% due to stress and the startle effect (Lewinski & Hudson, 2014). This means the already concerning 2.17-second response time could extend even further in real-world situations.

The research underscores that traditional range training may not adequately prepare officers for the speed and complexity of real-world armed encounters, particularly when a subject has already fired the initial shots. Fractions of a second count, and training must go beyond flat range marksmanship drills.

Evaluation of Tactical Movement and Firearm Draw Performance During Charging Knife Attacks

The present study has elaborated on the 21-ft principle (Tueller, 1983) and examined different attack distances with a knife, providing additional information on how fast a dynamic knife attack can occur and how fast law enforcement officers need to respond during these threats at different distances.

- Kantor et al., 2024

This 2024 study examined the performance of law enforcement officers in the face of a charging knife attack. A charging knife attack is an excellent example of the context in which speed and dynamic response are critical to winning. The results were exciting regarding the disparity between how the officers performed when the pressure of the situation changed. Their speed and technique were different when faced with even simulated danger versus when they provided baseline data. Their standard presentation and aiming protocols were abandoned in favor of an adaptation that allowed them to be faster and did not involve using sights!

The participants in this study were twenty law enforcement officers. Sixteen were male officers, four were female. They had an average of 13.5 years of service, and their average age was 36 years. The metrics measured in the study were firearm draw performance, the speed of trigger movement, and the efficacy of different movement tactics. Each officer completed three movement options at each distance. The movement options were:

- Stationary – the officer could not move their body from the starting point
- Lateral – the officer moved to their dominant side (right-handed shooters moved right, left-handed shooters moved left)
- Rearward – officers moved backward, keeping their torsos toward the attacker

The officers completed these movement drills four times, varying the distance from their attacker each time. They started at ten feet, then moved to fifteen, twenty-one, and thirty feet. They were required to fire two rounds at their attacker during each trial. They could begin their response when they saw their attacker move toward them. Before the assessment, each officer drew and fired two rounds under no attack to set a baseline for their draw and shooting speed. The draw performance was assessed using movement sensors attached to the officer's body. The time began when the officer moved to start their draw process; the time ended when they had fired their second round. The trigger cadence, or time between rounds, was also measured using sensors attached to the officer's body.

The knife attacker was a college-aged male; he was not aware of which movement tactic the officer would use to evade each attack. The knife attacker's timed movement began when his front foot lifted off the ground, and the time ended when any part of his body (including the knife) crossed the cone where the officer started the trial. The attacker was deemed to have contacted the officer when the knife passed their extended firearm. If contact was not made, the officer was considered to have survived that encounter. The overall survival rates broke down like this:

Distance from subject	Survival rate
10 feet	15%
15 feet	58%
21 feet	95%
30 feet	100%

This is not to say that any distance provides magical protective properties or guaranteed safety. What it does indicate is that distance matters. More distance translates to more time, increasing the officer's opportunity to assess and respond. The further away the officer was when the attack began, the greater their chance of effectively responding. That was probably not a revelation, but having research-backed data to support what is 'known' is helpful.

Another potentially expected outcome was that movement was advantageous. At ten, fifteen, and twenty-one feet, the officers who moved had a higher survival rate than the ones who remained stationary. The only trial where all the officers failed to have time to draw and fire was at ten feet with no movement – it had a 0% survival rate. Thirty feet was the only distance where officers had enough time to remain stationary. The overall movement survival rates were quite close when comparing rearward and lateral at each distance. Backward movement was slightly more successful overall, yielding a 72.5% survival rate. The lateral movement had a 71.25% survival rate. Terrain and context will determine which direction officers will move in an operational setting, but it seems clear that moving matters.

There was no statistically relevant difference in the speed at which the officers pressed the trigger. Despite the exigencies of the closer attacks, the time between shots was unchanged. The average times between shots at each distance were:

Distance from subject	Time between shots
10 feet	0.26 seconds
15 feet	0.23 seconds
21 feet	0.24 seconds
30 feet	0.25 seconds

The officers didn't or perhaps couldn't move the trigger any faster than they were doing. All the officers drew and shot faster when they were closer to the attacker, but the overall speed came from adjustments to their draw and aiming technique, not from moving the trigger quicker.

The speed at which the officers drew their guns was fascinating. All draw speeds in the knife attack trials were faster than the baselines, varying between 0.2 and 0.54 seconds faster. It seems that when the officers were placed under pressure, they worked faster than their 'normal' rate. As well as working faster, the other change in their process was how they presented and aimed the gun. The closer the officers were to their attacker, the less their draw and presentation looked like their baseline performance. The baseline shooting looked like a classic range stance. Their arms were fully extended, and the gun was brought up to eye level with a two-handed grip formed. During the proximity attacks, the officers shot from compressed positions with the handgun close to their torso and much lower than their eyeline. They were, without question, using a TFS approach to aim the gun. Based on the gun position, there is no way they could have seen their sights even if they had wanted to.

The officers were not instructed to adapt their technique, but this change aligns with commonly observed performances in high-stress time-compressed circumstances. Officers must abandon traditional 'range practice' techniques to match the speed of their response to the dynamic circumstances they find themselves in. This is one of the reasons that videos of officer-involved shootings look nothing like typical live fire range training sessions. It is another driving factor to reassess how we teach and prioritize speed of effective response in dynamic circumstances.

This study provides valuable empirical evidence that supports and expands upon the relevance of time and distance. The findings demonstrate three critical factors in officer survival during knife attacks: distance advantage, movement necessity, and adaptive technique under pressure. Officers performed significantly better with increased distance from the threat, dramatically improving survival rates from 15% at 10 feet to 100% at 30 feet; distance bought them time. Movement—lateral or rearward—proved essential to survival, particularly at closer distances where stationary positions resulted in significantly lower survival rates; movement bought them time.

Perhaps most importantly, the study reveals how officers naturally adapt their firearms techniques under threat conditions. The instinctive shift from traditional range shooting positions to compressed, close-to-body positions and a target-focused approach suggests that training protocols should incorporate these realistic pressure-induced responses rather than expecting officers to maintain static form during dynamic confrontations. Law enforcement training should focus on developing proficiency with compressed shooting positions, rapid target acquisition without reliance on sights, and deliberate integration of movement tactics during firearms training.

This research also underscores the importance of training with human opponents. Time compression and mobile opponents prepare officers to respond effectively when traditional techniques must give way to survival-focused adaptations.

Conclusion

The overwhelming evidence from multiple empirical studies points to an urgent need to reform traditional firearms training approaches. Current training methodologies, built primarily around static marksmanship and sight-focused shooting, fail to align with the physiological realities of close-quarter encounters and the demonstrated practices of elite performers (Morrison, 1998; Taylor, 2021). The research conclusively shows that in distances under 15 feet, where nearly half of all police shootouts occur, target-focused techniques offer superior decision-making quality and response speed (Lewinski et al., 2015).

The stakes could not be higher, with studies showing that naive shooters can draw and fire in as little as 0.38 seconds, and officer fatalities predominantly occur within the first few seconds of engagement (Kantor et al., 2022); every fraction of a second matters. Traditional sight-focused training methods can add critical delays of 0.30 seconds or more, which could prove fatal (Lewinski et al., 2015; Blair et al., 2016).

The evidence advocates for a fundamental shift in training priorities:

1. Emphasize target-focused shooting techniques for close-quarter encounters, allowing officers to maintain crucial visual contact with subjects and gather maximum information for decision-making (Taylor, 2021; Vickers & Lewinski, 2012).

2. Restructure initial firearms training to establish target-focused habits from the beginning rather than attempting to retrain officers later. Vickers and Lewinski's (2012) research demonstrates that early training patterns persist under stress.

3. Integrate realistic scenario-based training that incorporates the time pressures and decision-making demands of actual encounters, moving beyond traditional marksmanship qualifications that set an artificially low standard (Lewinski et al., 2015).

4. Acknowledge and work with, rather than against, the natural human tendency to maintain a visual focus on threats. Elite performers demonstrate this pattern, with up to 86% of final fixations on the threat during successful engagements (Vickers & Lewinski, 2012).

This evidence-informed approach promises multiple benefits: faster response times in critical situations, better threat assessment through unobstructed observation, and improved decision-making quality through maintained visual contact (Taylor, 2021). Most importantly, it aligns training with the actual dynamics of close-quarter encounters where officers must rapidly process information and respond while maintaining awareness of potential threats (Lewinski et al., 2014).

The research presents a clear mandate for change. While possibly valuable for basic marksmanship, traditional firearms training must evolve to better prepare officers for the realities of modern law enforcement encounters (Lewinski et al., 2015; Vickers & Lewinski, 2012). By embracing target-focused techniques and training methodologies that leverage natural physiological responses, we can better prepare officers for the split-second decisions they must make. Firearms are among the most significant levels of force officers deploy. Although the use of deadly force is rare (Bozeman et al., 2018), officers must be prepared for the possibility.

The time has come to move beyond tradition and dogma (Morrison, 1998) and embrace evidence-informed training approaches. The research shows us the way forward, but we must be courageous in following the path.

The research indicates that effective use of vision and attention is a highly influential factor in success. We need to know how each process works to understand the most effective ways to introduce the direction of vision and attention early in training.

CHAPTER 6 - VISION

"Reality" changes right before your eyes on many occasions. You walk into a movie theater during the day. It is very black and you can see little. After a while, your eyes adapt, the scene looks brighter and you can see much that was previously invisible. Which is the "real" world - the dark theater or the bright theater? The answer is obviously neither. Your brain created both.

- Marc Green

Vision is a fascinating and complex topic. There are still facets of how we process visual information being studied, and discoveries are being made to this day. For instance, did you know that how we see color is not certain? There are two main and differing theories for how we perceive color vision (Dawn M. McBride et al., 2022):

Trichromatic theory: the idea that color vision is accomplished through a pattern of activation across the three types of cones.

Opponent-process theory: the idea that color vision is accomplished through opponent-process cells that are excited or inhibited by pairs of colors.

The human body and brain are amazing and complex. The high-level overview here is focused on practitioners and trainers. This is not intended as a deep dive into human anatomy. If you are interested in digging deeper into any or all the concepts, the references included will allow expansion to a much greater degree. As trainers, we should understand the basic processes of vision.

How we absorb information to drive decision-making and how we use vision to carry out our selected responses to that information is tremendously important. We need to have a working knowledge of visual limitation, the duration of eye movement, and the effect that those movements have on the availability of information. This chapter will cover those aspects of vision and the parts of the eye that allow us to see. Once we've covered the function and rudimentary construction of the visual system, we'll move on to some of the trickery built into it and its relevance to TFS.

Vision Basics

The Cliff Notes version of how our eyes work goes like this. The eyes take in information in the form of light, which is converted into electrical signals, transmitted along the optic nerve, and processed by the brain. The processing that happens beyond the eyeball in the brain is not entirely relevant to what we are looking at here (pun intended). If we agree that visual information being processed by the brain comes via the eyeball(s), we have enough to get started.

How that light/information enters the eye is controlled by a few different parts of the eye. This is particularly relevant for shooters who are identifying targets or subjects that need to be assessed and potentially shot - or not. Our eyelids, first and foremost, need to be open to allow the eyeball to receive quality information. It's not uncommon for pistol shooters to try to close or partially close/squint one of their eyelids. With our eyelids fully closed or squinted/partially closed, we are limiting our information-gathering potential. With an eyelid closed, at best, we may be able to assess the perception of light or dark. Hindering the use of one of our eyes inhibits our ability to acquire information we may desperately need. We are designed to acquire maximum information with both eyes open. A system of shooting that allows and encourages both eyes to be open is preferred for this maximization.

Iris & Pupil

Working from the outside in, the first variable relevant to our discussion are the pupil and the iris (see Figure 1). The iris is the colored part of the eye, while the dark central area is the pupil. The pupil is the opening in the iris that allows light and information into the eye. The iris controls the size of the pupil. Many reasons explain why pupil size varies. One of the most well-known reasons for pupil size variation is to manage light entry levels. If light is bright, the pupil will be smaller; if it's dark, the pupil will be larger. Pupil size can also vary based on emotional arousal, cognitive task demands, and motor output (Fletcher et al., 2017). The human pupil can vary in diameter from less than 1 millimeter to more than 9 millimeters (Beatty & Lucero-Wagner, 2000). We will discuss pupil size and iris changes later; for now, knowing what they are, and their locations is all we need.

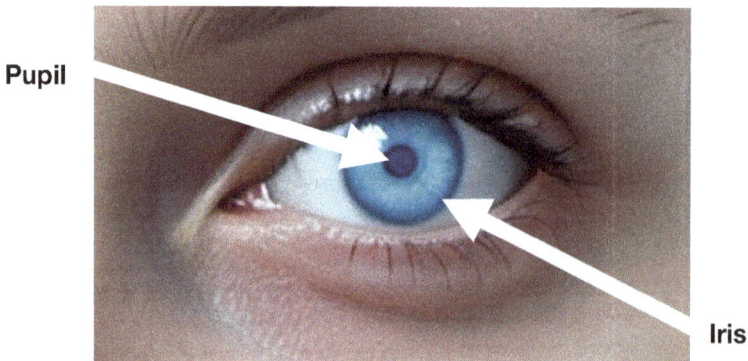

Figure 1 *Image of human eye with pupil and iris labeled*

Lens

The lens (see Figure 2) sits behind the pupil, suspended by small muscles called ciliary muscles. The lens is flexible, and the ciliary muscles change its shape to adapt it to the task at hand. When you focus on something far away, the lens is shaped differently than when you focus on something close. The ciliary muscles alter the lens shape by stretching it (or not) to refract light and enable us to focus our vision.

Ciliary muscles stretch the lens thin when we focus on something at a distance. When we are focusing on something close, the ciliary muscles relax and allow the lens to thicken. Without this adaptation, we could not focus our vision clearly on objects.

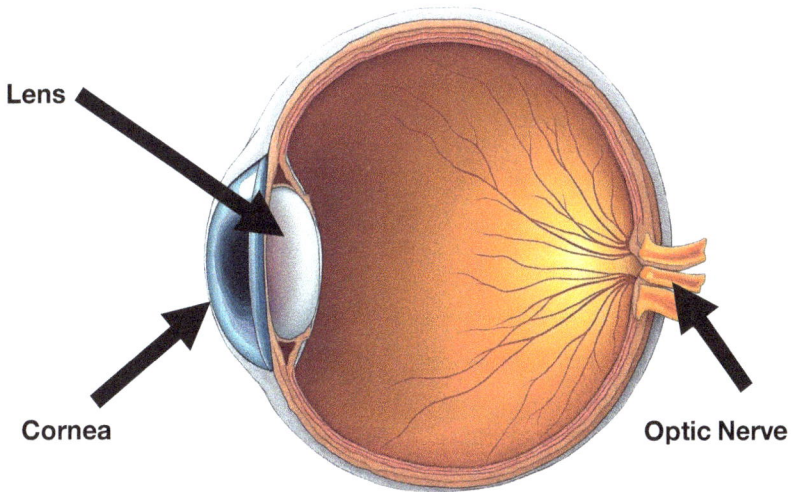

Lens

Cornea

Optic Nerve

Figure 2 *Image showing cross-section of the human eyeball with lens, cornea, and optic nerve labelled*

Retina and Blind Spot

The retina is the area on the back of the eyeball with the image "projected" onto it by light passing through the lens. The retina is lined with receptor cells called rods and cones. Rods allow us to see (poorly) in the dark. They are most prevalent on the edge of the cornea. Cones are the receptors that give us the clearest vision. Cones are concentrated most densely in the retina's center in an area called the macula. In the center of the macula is a smaller area packed with nothing but cones. This small area is called the fovea.

Although we perceive everything out in front of us as being equally clear and visible, this is an illusion. Our only true high-clarity vision is projected onto the fovea. This foveal vision accounts for only a few degrees of our visual world. It provides us with the greatest visual clarity. If you want to get an idea of how big, or perhaps I should say small, an area foveal vision represents, extend your arm and look at your thumbnail. Your thumbnail is roughly the size of your foveal vision at that distance.

The rest of our visual area has poorer clarity, and believe it or not, there are areas out in front of you where you have no vision at all. Actual blind spots exist due to no receptors on the retina. These areas with no receptors or blind spots are created by the presence of the optic nerve (see Figure 2). Your brain, in its helpful wisdom, fills in the blank spots for you so you do not realize they are there. There are some ways to expose the trickery, though, if accepting this to be true is a challenge, with just two thumbs, we can figure this out:

How to Find a Blind Spot

Right eye blind spot

Close your left eye.

Hold your left thumb out in front of you, with your arm straight.

Place your right thumb next to your left thumb.

Look at your left thumb with your right eye.

Slowly move your right thumb to the right while looking at your left thumb.

When your right thumb disappears, you found your right eye's blind spot.

Left eye blind spot

Close your right eye.

Hold your right thumb out in front of you, with your arm straight.

Place your left thumb next to your right thumb.

Look at your right thumb with your left eye.

Slowly move your left thumb to the left while looking at your right thumb.

When it disappears, you found your left eye's blind spot.

How big is the blind spot?

When you find the blind spot move your thumb up and down, and to the left and right. It will appear and disappear as you find the limits of that blind spot.

Saccades & Smooth Pursuits

Now that we have uncovered one area of trickery where our brain leads us to believe we have complete uninterrupted vision, let's explore another. That small area of concentrated cones called the fovea provides us with our clearest vision. As you read this text, you direct your foveal vision across the page to the subsequent words. If you look down at the page number, then back to this line of text, the eye movement that allows you to do so is called a saccade. You are using saccadic movements when you look around a room or to the rearview mirror as you drive. Saccades are discrete jumps of the eye that direct the center of your gaze to different parts of the world (Bisley, 2020). Saccades are small eye movements, typically less than 10 degrees of visual angle (Hagan et al., 2020). If you were making a bigger visual adjustment, say off the page and over your shoulder that would need a head movement too. That visual change would still include a saccade – probably preceding the head motion (Hagan et al., 2020). You have experienced saccadic movement thousands of times and, more often than not, probably do not notice. The reason for so much eye movement is to maximize the availability of the rich cluster of cells on the fovea. We shift our eyes around constantly to direct that finite tunnel of high-definition visual acuity to what we are trying to focus on. Saccades go largely unnoticed by our conscious mind. We visually scan around a room, and the information flow seems unbroken. Our brain is deceiving us once more.

When we move our eyes, information is not available for processing by our brain. This loss of information is measured anywhere from 0.3 to 0.5 seconds (Manning & Riggs, 1984). It is called saccadic suppression. Just as our brain pastes over our blind spot to create the illusion of seeing uninterruptedly, it does the same with saccades. We do not notice the loss. As saccades take place, the visual field can be manipulated, and the changes go unnoticed.

As we saccade our vision around our environment, our blind spot moves around, too. It occupies the same position in relation to what we are looking at, but as we change what we're focusing our foveal vision on, the blind spot falls on a different area of our environment. Each time we focus on something in a new location, we give up adjacent visual information.

Saccades allow us to move our vision from one area to another, but we have a different process for tracking a moving target. If we look at something that is moving and continue to track it while it moves, this eye movement is termed a smooth pursuit. A smooth pursuit is a slower eye movement than saccades. Saccades are a fast jump from one area to another, sometimes called a ballistic movement. While tracking a moving object, we can consistently sustain it within our foveal vision until or unless we saccade to a new target.

Saccadic movement takes time to initiate and to complete. It can take .15 - .4 seconds to initiate a saccade following the presentation of the stimulus (van Zoest et al., 2017). This time span can be affected by the distance of the saccade, the prominence of the stimulus, and whether the eye movement is accurate. If the saccade is larger, for instance, if the distance between where we are looking and where we are going to look is greater, the initiation of the movement tends to be slower. Similarly, if the stimulus isn't prominent or conspicuous, the initiation of eye movement is also typically slower. Furthermore, if we are intentionally moving our eyes to something, this process is typically slower than if our attention is drawn to an irrelevant stimulus.

Transitioning Focus Distance

Adjusting our focus distance from near to far or vice versa requires several muscular movements. This transition is one of the most relevant eye movements when deciding whether to remain target-focused or focus on the gun when aiming.

The expected process for using pistol sights involves identifying a target, potentially deciding whether it needs to be shot, and then looking at the front sight to aim that shot or shots. A relevant example of this would be a shooter who is looking at a subject or target 15 feet away and then shifting their visual focus to their firearm, which is at arm's length. If we choose to change our focus of vision from far to near or vice versa, three physical changes must occur with our eyes. The movements are opposites depending on which direction we are going. I will break these down further, but for a starting reference, the three movements to shift visual focus from far to near are as follows:

- Convergence
- Pupillary Constriction
- Accommodation

As with all bodily movements, they take time. Like a saccade, we suppress information intake during the process, too. There are a few different terms used for this combination of movements, such as the near response, the near triad (Mays & Gamlin, 1995), the accommodation reflex, the near reflex, or the accommodation-convergence reflex (Motlagh & Geetha, 2022). For simplicity, I will use the term accommodation reflex for the example above. When deciding to shift focus from the target to sights, an accommodation reflex is required to make that happen. Each of the movements breaks down like this.

Vergence

Vergence movements align the fovea with objects at different distances. They refer to the simultaneous and coordinated movement of the eyes to obtain or maintain focus. They are classified as convergence and divergence.

Unlike saccades and smooth pursuits, the eyes do not move in the same direction for vergence. They rotate toward one another for close vision (convergence) or away from one another to adjust to focus at a distance (divergence).

The eye muscles responsible for this convergence and divergence are called the extraocular muscles. As we shift our gaze between near and far objects, these muscles continuously adjust the position of the eyes to maintain appropriate vergence for the task.

Convergence - Focusing on something up close requires the eyes to converge. This involves each eyeball directing the irises toward one another. If you've ever seen someone look at their own nose, you've encountered an extreme example of the direction I am referring to (see Figure 3).

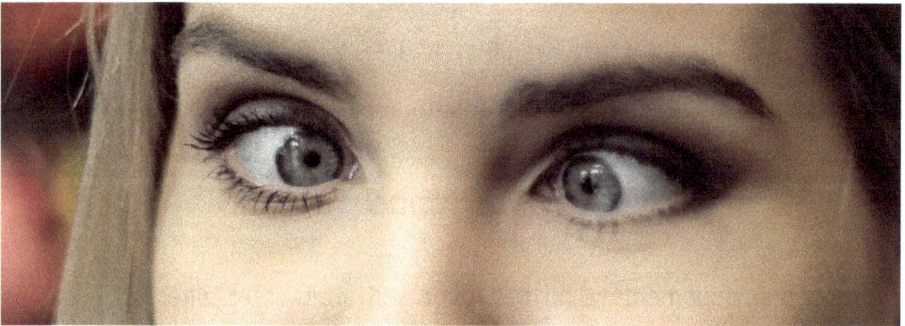

Figure 3 *Image of eyes converging*

Divergence - Focusing on something further away requires the divergence of the eyes. The eyes shift the iris away from the nose when we adjust our vision to look at objects that are far from us. This opposing movement is called divergence.

If a shooter tries to shift their focus from their sights to a distant object or target, the movement will be divergence. When they return their vision from the distant object back to the sights, the movement will be convergence. Vergence is essential for depth perception and accurately judging objects' distance and relative positions in our visual field. The automatic control of the extraocular muscles is a key part of the eye's focusing capabilities.

Vergence causes the same visual suppression as a saccade or a blink. Potentially inhibiting information for .3 - .4 seconds (Manning, 1986), (Hung et al., 1990) .3 - .5 seconds (Manning & Riggs, 1984).

Pupillary Constriction

Our pupil size is different for an object at two feet versus an object at twenty feet. Pupillary constriction is the process by which the pupil (the opening in the center of the iris) becomes smaller in size. This change occurs when we view objects from different distances.

The pupil constricts to a smaller size (see Figure 4) when looking at something up close, around arm's length - like the sights on a pistol. This constriction helps focus the light entering the eye and improves the depth of the field for near objects. Conversely, when looking at distant objects around twenty feet away or more, the pupil dilates or expands to a larger size (see Figure 5). This allows more light to enter the eye, improving visibility and focus on faraway objects.

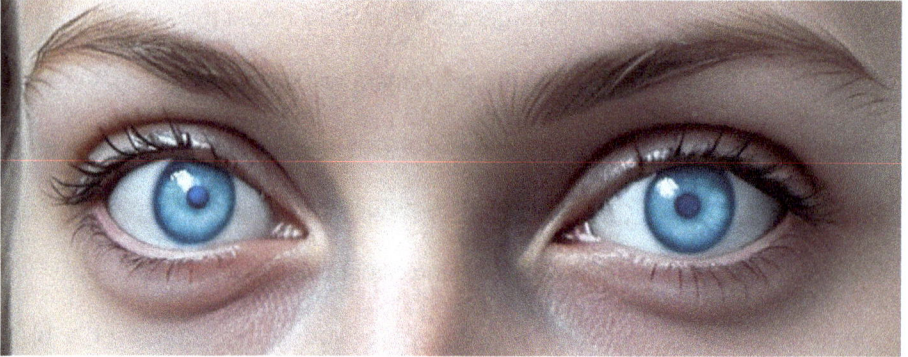

Figure 4 Image of eyes with constricted pupils

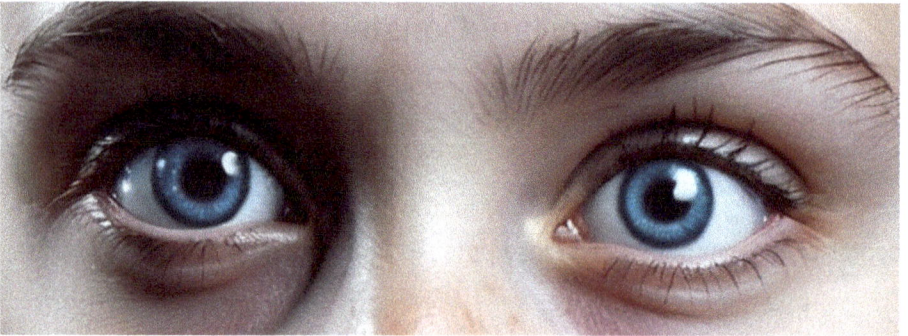

Figure 5 Image of eyes with dilated pupils

The autonomic nervous system controls pupillary constriction and dilation. These actions happen automatically as we shift our gaze between near and far objects. This dynamic pupil adjustment is essential to the eye's overall focusing mechanism.

Pupils don't just dilate when intending to look at something at a distance; they also dilate when aroused. Whether that arousal is due to a visual or an auditory stimulus seems to make little difference (Bradley et al., 2008). Our emotional reaction to our environment can adjust our pupil size without our control, just the same way our heart rate may increase, and we may get sweaty palms. We don't consciously initiate these physiological responses to arousal (Mathôt, 2018; Alshak & Das, 2023).

Accommodation

Directly behind the iris and pupil is the eye's crystalline lens. The lens is one of the eye's essential refractive elements. The lens changes shape through a process called accommodation. Ciliary muscles control the lens's shape change (Benarroch, 2014). The ciliary muscles are small, ring-shaped muscles located just behind the iris. The ciliary muscles are essential for allowing us to focus our vision and shift that visual focus as needed. Our lens must be pulled thin when we look at a potential target at a distance. When we shift visual focus to the gun at arm's length, the lens must bulge and thicken (see Figure 6).

a. Distant object

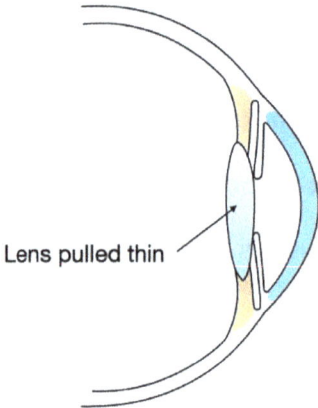

b. Near object

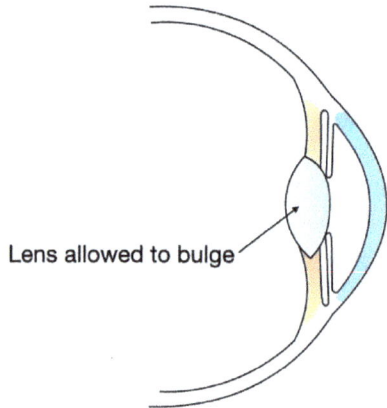

Figure 6 a. Cross-section image of the eye, showing the lens pulled thin to focus on a distant object. *b*. Cross-section image of the eye, showing the lens allowed to bulge to focus on a close object

Controlling Vision

In addition to the multiple muscle-driven physical changes required to move our visual focus from one place to another, the ability to stop looking at one object and shift our visual focus to another also requires two actions by the brain. For example, find a spot where you can look at a picture or a television on the wall across a room. Then, extend one of your hands out in front of you and point up toward the ceiling so you can see the nail of that finger. Align your finger so it appears to be between you and the object you have selected (see Figure 7).

Figure 7 *Image showing a picture in the distance in clear focus; there is an extended index finger in the foreground of the image that is slightly out of focus, displaying the reality that we can only focus on one object at a time.*

You can see both the finger and the object across the room at the same time, but you cannot focus on both at once. You must choose. Without head movement, we can move our eyes and shift our focus to what we see clearly. That shift from one object to another appears to be an instantaneous action. However, it is not quite so simple. We first need to let go of our fixation on one object, such as the picture on the wall. Then we move our gaze to the other object, like our finger. Our brain must prepare to relinquish one focus and initiate attention on the other. While the switching occurs simultaneously, the preparation for both can be measured as reaction time (Reppert et al., 2018).

An everyday example of the delay between the perception of stimuli and the response can be found in driving. Seeing a car unexpectedly brake in front of you means you need to use your own brakes. The time between the perception of the brake lights of the vehicle ahead of you and the initiation of moving your foot is called reaction time. It may be short or long, but reaction time is the measurable period between the stimulus and the start of the response (see Figure 8). This is another hidden layer of complexity to our intricate visual system and processes.

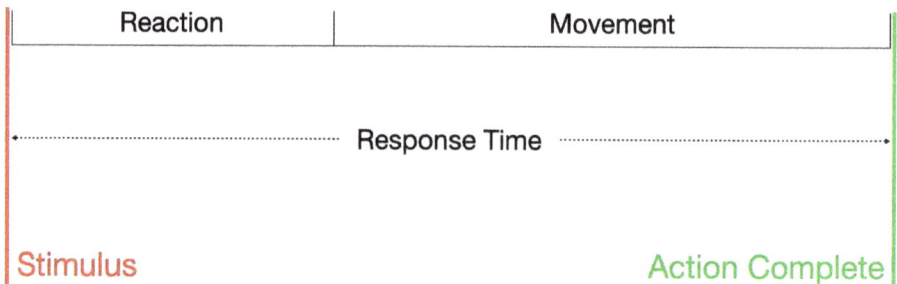

Reaction	Movement

Response Time

Stimulus   Action Complete

Figure 8 Diagram showing that the response time between a stimulus and the completion of an action is broken down into reaction and response time

Conclusion

...under stress, attention is directed toward the threatening stimuli, rather than task-relevant processes.

- Baldwin et al., 2022

Adjusting what we are looking at takes time—it is a measurable event. Research provides specific time spans for each of these visual adjustments, some of which overlap. While these times vary based on individuals and operational context, one certainty remains: this all takes time.

Adjusting our visual focus also causes a temporary loss of visual information, like closing your eyes completely (see saccades and saccadic suppression). As trainers and practitioners, we must consider how trade-offs in reaction time and information loss shape decision quality and performance. These should be foundational principles that drive our choices in techniques we endorse and the precious time we invest in practice.

Decision-based shooting differs fundamentally from range-based shooting. Losses of visual information may go unnoticed on the range; those losses are particularly impactful to decision-making. At the range, shooters know what to shoot and when, this is normally made very clear before practice begins. In life-threatening situations involving deadly force, the decisions of when and what to shoot are influenced by external factors (refer to top-down and bottom-up processing for more details). Most often, the sources of these decision-making cues are rooted in vision. We see and perceive the threat, applying force until we determine the threat is neutralized. Information about subject behavior and actions tends to be primarily vision-based. We observe the person, object, and environment to determine if an immediate threat exists. If we attempt to shift our visual focus from that subject back to the sighting system, information is suppressed, and time is lost. Both information loss and time delay are potentially detrimental to our task. An additional challenge may be our physical inability to focus on something at close range.

When we experience arousal or fear, our sympathetic nervous system automatically initiates bodily changes. Digestion stops, heart rate increases, and—importantly for this chapter—the eyes are also automatically affected. The radial muscles of our pupil contract, causing mydriasis (Alshak & Das, 2023). Mydriasis is the technical term for pupil dilation, meaning our pupil size increases, allowing more light to enter the eye and enhancing distance vision. The dilated pupil enables us to see clearly from 7 meters to infinity (Mathôt, 2018). This visual shift is sometimes called optical infinity (Honig, 2008). The ciliary muscles that control the lens also relax, further enhancing our ability to see at a distance (Alshak & Das, 2023).

These changes in the eye represent our body's automatic attempt to increase our ability to see objects at greater distances. These vision changes may explain why many officers never see their tiny sights (Artwohl & Christensen, 1997), or if they do, perceive only a blur or "splotch" (Spaulding, 2024). Vision is not hardwired to focus optimally at arm's length or closer when we are in fear. We were not designed to examine objects in our hands when our lives are in danger. We are preparing for fight or flight—looking at what threatens us enough to require lethal force or searching for an escape route.

Your life to this point has probably been measured in years. In an exchange of close-quarter violence, the rest of your life may be measured in fractions of a second. Do you want to take the time to stop looking at your opponent at bad breath distance? Do you need to take that time? Do you have that time?

CHAPTER 7 - ATTENTION

Attention is a broad term that refers to the various ways we allocate our limited cognitive resources to the current task at hand.

- McBride et al., 2023

Attention is a finite resource; we only have so much available at any given time. Knowing when and where to direct it is crucial. Attentional focus is also a learned process that should be considered in all aspects of training, though it is often overlooked or assumed to be understood by our learners.

Many factors impact the attentional bandwidth we have available to us, including the task's complexity and our familiarity with it. For example, think about the first time a child begins to walk independently. Aside from the immense physical feat this is for them, consider how focused their attention is. Every part of their body and mind is focused on this task. Their balance suffers when that attentional focus is broken when a toy catches their eye, and gravity pulls them back to earth. Now, think about how many mental and physical tasks you undertake daily while walking around. The amount of conscious attention you pay to the physical act of walking is minimal, if any.

Knowing what needs your attention and what doesn't comes from practice. Focusing attention is a learned process. This is especially relevant when training people to assess complex situations and potentially make decisions about life-saving uses of force. Seasoned professionals know where to direct attention to maximize their informational gathering potential, as the research highlighted in the previous chapter demonstrates. Now that we know that is the case, shouldn't we be trying to close the skill gap of attentional focus between the novice and the expert?

A simple way to highlight how attentional focus can impact the speed of processing is the Stroop Task. It's not related to shooting, but it's a great everyday example of how a well-practiced process can become subconsciously efficient. It also clearly illustrates how performance on a simple task can suffer due to the inherent drain of attentional focus.

The original study, completed in 1935, was called the "Name the color or word test, where the color of the print and the word are different" (Stroop, 1935). The title described the task clearly. However, it is a bit of a mouthful. It has commonly become known as the Stroop Test or Stroop Task, named after the test designer, J. Ridley Stroop. The rules are simple, but the task can be surprisingly mentally demanding. From top to bottom, list the color of the shape in column I and record the time taken to do so. Repeat the task for the color of the lettering in columns II and III (see Figure 9).

I	II	III
★	Red	Green
★	Yellow	Orange
★	Brown	Yellow
★	Green	Black
★	Blue	Red
★	Orange	Blue
★	Black	Brown

Figure 9 Stroop test example

When looking at the symbols in column I, naming the color and paying little attention to the shape's form does not tax our attention. The same is common for column II. As we look at the lettering, we read the word and the word coincides with the color. The time is usually very similar to that for column I. The stumbling block for most people (including me) comes when we get to column III. It usually takes longer because we need to 'stop' ourselves from reading the words. Skilled readers cannot shut off the automatic process of reading. We have learned to effortlessly direct our attention to perceiving the shape of letters and forming them into words.

The people who slowdown in column III display the result of learned attentional focus. In what seems an effortless and subconscious process, they begin to read the words without trying or wanting to. Our lifetime of reading and associated learned application of attention come into play automatically.

If you complete the Stroop task with young children who have not yet become skilled readers, you will not see the same disparity with column III. This further highlights the learned nature of unconscious task completion, sometimes referred to as automaticity. In contrast, Stroop also showed in his research that when already skilled readers practice the task, they can improve their times for column III. This affirms that attentional focus is something that can be trained. We can take a controlled process and make it automatic. Attention can be trained, and our processing times can be improved; automaticity is a key element of maximizing minimal resources.

Varying the Demands on Attention Through Automaticity

As we anchor skills and develop automaticity, we free up attentional resources. Driving is a notable everyday example of how automaticity helps. Driving also serves as an example of attentional limitation. When someone first learns to drive, it is an attention-guzzling task. A new driver's attentional resources are consumed with operating the vehicle and moving through the world around them. As the driver's experience, skill, and confidence grow, the task of driving becomes less demanding on their attention.

An easy drive to a familiar place in light traffic poses relatively low demand for a skilled driver. However, changing the context of the skill application can change the attentional demands required to complete it. If that same driver were in an unfamiliar rental vehicle in high-speed traffic in a city they do not know, and for the full effect, it was also dark and raining, things would be different. While the driver may still be fully capable of operating the vehicle and reaching their destination, doing so will demand significantly greater attentional resources to ensure safe navigation.

We tend to overestimate our attentional ability. There is often an illusion that attentional capacity is greater than it actually is. Driving can also be an everyday example of this. Cell phone use is the modern cause of many vehicle collisions. Look around during transit; drivers frequently and unashamedly operate their phones and stare at the screens while driving. This is an overtaxing of attentional resources (Strayer et al., 2003); we have laws and traffic crash statistics to prove it. Staring at the phone while driving links nicely to our next attentional delusion, multitasking.

The Myth of Multitasking

The myth of multitasking is a strong one. It is not accurate to completely dismiss multitasking as impossible. To some degree, it is possible to do multiple things at once. If one task is honed to automaticity, it may take an extremely low toll on our attentional capacity. You could no doubt stand on one foot and read this book. However, the tasks' relative complexity plays a part in the quality of our performance. Our bandwidth of attentional resources is finite. Multitasking essentially divides that limited attentional resource; it might be better described as switch tasking, as we rapidly and repeatedly bounce our attention from doing one thing to another.

If you have a lifetime of walking skills accrued, you can walk and chew gum or walk and hold a conversation. You may even be able to turn your head and look in a different direction toward the person walking alongside you while you walk and talk, for example. Would walking be so simple if you were told to do it on a narrow rope hundreds of feet up in the air (see Figure 10)? Would you be casually having the same conversation? Would you dare to turn your head? The complexity of putting one foot in front of the other would become an attentional drain. Your resources would be devoted to balance and survival!

How about walking the tightrope backward while listing all prime numbers from 1 to 100? The more novel and demanding the tasks, the more significant the decrease in our performance of them en masse. During this high attentional demand, when massive amounts of information are available but too overwhelming to process, attentional filtering comes into play.

Figure 10 *Image of a person walking across a tightrope*

Attentional Filtering

...there is no conscious perception without attention.

- Simons & Chabris, 1999

More sensory information is available at any given moment than we can consciously process. Our attentional bandwidth cannot handle the volume of data available, so we filter. Things inside and outside our bodies are always available to us as perceivable input from our senses; we routinely filter most of it out. Here are a couple of everyday sensory examples.

Vision - most of you can see some part of your nose. Go ahead and take a look. It is always there, yet until just now, you had not been paying attention to it.

Touch - If you are wearing glasses right now, there is pressure on your nose and ears that you probably overlooked. If you are sitting down as you read, pressure is on your body from your seat. Hopefully, you are wearing clothes as you read- the contact of your clothing on your skin is ever-present. Your tongue feels some part of your mouth, but you do not notice it as you read. Vast volumes of sensory data are available anytime; you're just not always attending to it.

You can think of attentional filtering as a funnel. Despite the abundance of information, only a limited amount can be processed at any given time. The funnel effect also means that when we attend to one thing, it comes at the cost of not attending to other things. When you looked at your nose in amazement a few moments ago, you were no longer looking at the book. When thinking about the pressure on your skin from your clothes, you were not thinking about the words on this page. The funnel and filtering phenomenon leads us to our next topic, inattentional blindness.

Inattentional Blindness

Without attention, we often do not see unanticipated events; even with attention, we cannot encode and retain all the details of what we see.

- Simons & Chabris, 1999

A striking demonstration of perceptual filtering, particularly in the context of vision and attention, is inattentional blindness. The word blindness seems dramatic, but people with normal visual ability are functionally blind to large objects and unexpected changes. They do not see them, and as such, they are deemed blind to them (Koivisto et al., 2004). The most famous example of inattentional blindness is commonly referred to as the "Gorilla effect." This aptly nicknamed experiment tasked observers with watching a video of two groups of basketball players and counting the number of passes made by one of the groups. Approximately half of the observers failed to notice a person dressed in a gorilla costume walking amongst the players. The gorilla was onscreen for nine seconds, stopped in the middle of the players, faced the camera, and beat its chest before walking away. (Simons & Chabris, 1999).

The blindness phenomenon is not restricted to when something is added to the scene. It can also be applied when something changes in the scene. This is termed "change blindness" and relates to changes in our environment that we fail to perceive. Just like inattentional blindness, the researchers use the word "blind" to drive home just how exclusionary the effect is to us. Change blindness has the same dramatic influence on perception. Our failure to see the change renders us blind to that change.

Imagine that someone approached you asking for directions, and halfway through the conversation, when you provided those directions, someone else passed between you and the person seeking information. Your view was momentarily obscured. When the obstruction passes, the person you were talking to disappears, and someone else takes their place. That sounds like an easy change to spot, right? If the person who asked you for directions was different than the person who finished receiving the directions, you would notice. Possibly not. Experimenters did that swap, and as you may not be surprised to hear by now, attention was the flaw that left the subject of the experiment blind to the change. More than half of the experiment participants failed to notice that the person they were talking to was substituted halfway through their conversation (Simons & Levin, 1998).

The research into inattentional blindness in the late 1990s was made famous by the gorilla appearing in an unexpected place. That Gorilla principle was put into practice during another experiment years later called The Invisible Gorilla Strikes Again: Sustained Inattentional Blindness in Expert Observers (Drew et al., 2013). Researchers tasked radiologists with reviewing CT scans of lungs for cancer screening. The radiologists were considered to be experts at this task. Interleaved among the standard CT scans they reviewed were CT scans with images of a Gorilla embedded into them. Of the twenty-four radiologists tasked with assessing the scans, only four of them spotted the Gorilla. Eye tracking showed that more than half of the radiologists who didn't 'see' the Gorilla looked directly at its location when it was visible! This would support Simons and Charbris' earlier conclusion:

Objects can pass through the spatial extent of attentional focus (and the fovea) and still not be 'seen' if they are not explicitly being attended (1999).

It is possible to look and not see, just as it is possible to hear and not to listen. Some of you may think these experiments don't particularly apply to law enforcement professionals. What do Gorillas, basketballs, and CT scans have to do with anything? Cops are not immune to these limitations, as shown in a 2017 traffic stop experiment by Simons and Schlosser.

One of the most dangerous things a patrol officer does is engage in traffic stops. It is a known high-risk task, and during this event, when massive amounts of information are available, inattentional blindness is relevant and evident. Simons and Schlosser tasked one hundred and seventy-five police officers to conduct a simulated traffic stop. The participants were a mix of recruits and experienced officers, and inattentional blindness was still a prominent issue.

The experimenters placed a handgun in plain view on the dashboard of the vehicle driven by the subject of the traffic stop. More than half of the recruits failed to notice the gun. A third of the experienced officers failed to see it, too. Though the dashboard may not be the most common place to store a gun - it is undoubtedly more relevant to the task at hand than a Gorilla in a basketball game, and the limitations of attentional capacity were readily evident.

In this experiment and the other inattentional blindness research, the people who experienced it were frequently surprised to find out what they had 'missed' (Levin & Angelone, 2008; Simons & Schlosser, 2017). This disbelief is seemingly a common reaction; some participants are so convinced it did not happen to them that they need to see video evidence. Inattentional blindness is not something intuitively appreciated. Our perception of our ability to handle vast amounts of information, along with our misunderstanding of how much we can take in at any given moment, is seemingly skewed.

It is essential to acknowledge that inattentional blindness is a prevalent phenomenon that typically escapes conscious detection, making its consideration critical in designing and evaluating training programs. Sweeping statements like "Keep your head on a swivel" or "Have good situational awareness" are espoused by those who do not fully grasp how looking and seeing are separate processes. They both involve different mechanisms to manage bandwidth (attentional filtering-looking; inattentional blindness-seeing), while also limiting attentional capacity. The fragility and the interrelated nature of vision and attention should drive our decisions around how we apply the juxtaposition of vision and attention in our training approach. Nothing can be assumed.

The phenomenon of inattentional blindness challenges our fundamental assumptions about human perception and attention. While we might believe that we see everything in our field of vision, especially obvious threats, research tells a different story. Just as participants in the famous gorilla experiment failed to notice a person in a gorilla suit, officers can miss critical details (such as guns in plain view) when their cognitive resources are devoted to specific tasks, like a traffic stop. This selective attention process, driven by high perceptual load, can significantly impact an officer's ability to detect unexpected but potentially critical stimuli in their environment.

Attention is fragile and finite; if officers concentrate on a sighting system, they may become blind to other crucial details in their environment, including variances in the subject's intent, ability, or opportunity. Remaining target-focused for as long as possible, whenever possible, increases the likelihood of assimilating task-relevant information. Looking at the gun or its sights does nothing to aid decision-making. In fact, the more attention we pay to the gun, the fewer attentional resources we have available to decide if we need it. This concept highlights the critical need to understand how attention is classified.

Internal and External Attention

We can direct or focus our attention on different areas, places, or things. To broadly establish a starting point for this discussion, we could classify our attentional focus as internal or external. Of course, within those two expansive categories of classification, there are further subsections, such as broad or narrow (Nideffer & Sharpe, 1978). In table format, this high-level overview of attentional direction would look like this:

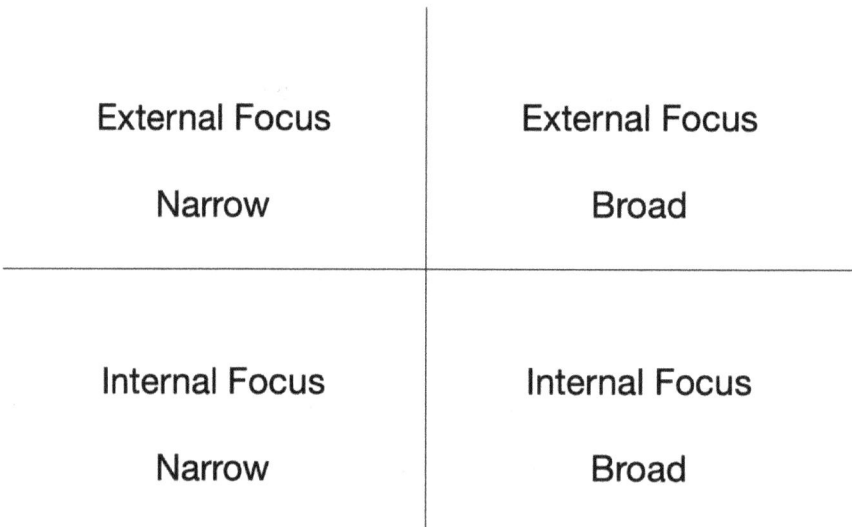

External Focus Narrow	External Focus Broad
Internal Focus Narrow	Internal Focus Broad

Figure 11 *Diagram showing quadrants of attention, external narrow, external broad, internal narrow, and internal broad*

Internal focus of attention

Internal focus of attention ties back to some of the earlier examples regarding attentional filtering. If you recall, it was suggested that your tongue always offers sensational information but is often filtered out of attentional focus. If you pay attention to it now, you will not only realize that you have been ignoring it as you frequently do, but you will also focus your attention internally. How your body feels, your thoughts, ideas, and emotions are all internal events occurring within your body. If you direct your focus to these areas, that is classified as an internal focus of attention.

External focus of attention

On the opposite end of the attentional scale is an external focus of attention. Paying attention to what is outside our body falls neatly into this category. Recalling our driving example from earlier in the chapter, when operating a vehicle, paying attention to the road ahead and the people around us as we navigate our way safely on a journey is a pronounced external focus of attention.

Attention can be drawn to and fro. It can bounce between internal and external. We can also direct our attention to more effectively accomplish tasks. Driving on a busy highway while trying to concentrate on feeling a piece of food stuck in your teeth with your tongue is a poor allocation of attentional resources. Equally, if you were trying to think of an ingenious solution to a novel problem but also trying to listen to an important speech at a seminar, you would not be on the way to achieving the best results for either task. Internal and external focus can be further sub-classified into narrow and broad.

Narrow focus

An external narrow focus of attention is an optimal way to realize success in many realms. In basketball, for example, there is no point in attending to the whole court when the time comes for a free throw. Your chosen point of reference on the basketball hoop should be all-consuming (Vickers, 2007). A narrow external focus of attention is advantageous for aiming in many sporting tasks, such as golf, baseball, soccer, etc. (Vickers, 2007).

In a shooting sense, this is often captured in the phrase "aim small, miss small." The adage goes: If you aim at someone's shirt button, you might miss by two inches. If you aim at the whole shirt, you might miss by two feet. There is no peer-reviewed research on those two measurements, but the theory that a narrow external focus of attention is advantageous for skill execution is sound (Lewinski, 2008). The downside of a narrow external focus of attention is perceptual narrowing. In a visual sense, you may have heard this referred to as tunnel vision. Intentionally creating a prolonged, narrow external focus is akin to self-inducing tunnel vision. A narrowed perceptual field may be, to say the least, suboptimal and potentially disastrous if left unchecked.

Broad focus

Returning to our sporting examples may help illustrate the advantage of a broad external focus of attention. When a basketball game is in full swing, it is far more critical for players to be broadly aware of where multiple key players are positioned. This broad external focus may include awareness of their teammates and the opposing team. In a fast-paced game, this will likely be a continually evolving scene. Focusing narrowly on something static, like the rim of the basket or even the ball, will not contribute to success.

In shooting, a narrow focus might be optimal for aiming and maybe a path to success in controlled environments or target practice (see closed skills). In more dynamic circumstances or operational applications, a broader external focus of attention is more appropriate for information gathering and decision-making. Narrow and broad are terms on a sliding scale (see Figure 12), ranging from the shirt button at one end, which would be narrow, to the entire crowd at a stadium event, which would be broad.

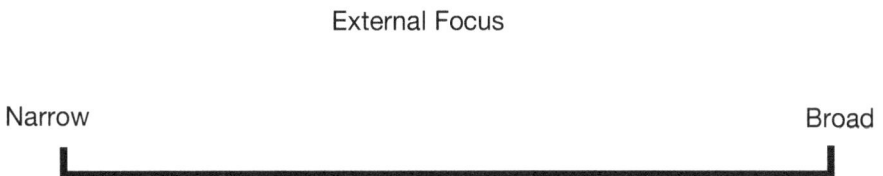

External Focus

Narrow   Broad

Figure 12 Diagram showing scale of external focus from narrow to broad

Optimal decision-making, as demonstrated in research, involves knowing where to look and when to look there (Vickers & Lewinski, 2012). More experienced officers knew how to direct their attention, where to focus it, and when to do so for improved decision-making and skill execution.

There is a time and a place for directing attention narrowly and broadly. As trainers, we need to understand what each of these terms means and how to create training that facilitates exploring the process. For example, a person learning a new physical skill may benefit from an internal focus of attention as they figure out the task. They shouldn't stay perpetually focused internally, or this will become their habit. A seasoned professional is more likely to underperform and choke if they remain internally focused during their performance (Lee, 2011).

The training we provide needs to build an understanding of the processes and the opportunity to practice those skills in contextually relevant circumstances. Training that involves watching a scene unfold and deciding if the need to shoot exists has a significantly higher chance of building transferable skills than mindlessly punching holes in paper to prepare for a test of that same pointless skillset. Our preparation is to prevail and protect life, not to score points – training needs to be built with that in mind. A critical part of prevailing involves understanding how real-world environments influence our perception and our decision-making.

Top-down and Bottom-up Attention

Our environment and the task at hand influence our decisions. Attention is not always consciously directed. Some stimuli override our conscious attention and snatch our focus from what we are currently engaged in. Imagine that you are reading this in a coffee shop or a cafe, quietly sipping your caffe latte and looking good.

This absolute page-turner of a text is enthralling you, and you do not want to put it down. The process by which you are attending to reading is termed top-down attention. If a group of armed robbers burst into the tranquil scene, firing guns, demanding money, and throwing fellow patrons to the floor, they would become the focus of your attention without needing to make the switch consciously. That would be bottom-up attention. Let us explore each process more.

Top-down

Top-down attention, also known as effortful, endogenous, or sustained attention, is the concentration we choose to devote to something, like reading a fantastic book!

Top-down attention is dominant in our everyday lives. Common activities such as learning, cooking, driving, and talking rely heavily on our top-down attentional processes. Choosing to direct our attention to tasks is essential for survival. If your ancestors had not used their top-down attentional direction to hunt for food, you would not be here now. Top-down attention can be just as useful for recreation as survival. Academic or professional success is likely heavily founded on top-down attention.

Law enforcement training is a very top-down process. Everything from field stripping a firearm, cleaning and even shooting defined drills on a range comfortably fall into top-down attentional processes. The prevalence of this type of attention use in training is often disassociated with the operational requirements of the practiced skill. Some of the most demanding elements of law enforcement work do not involve us effortfully applying attention. The most terrifying and demanding moments occur when our environment grabs our attention without effort.

Bottom-up

Bottom-up attention, also called automatic, exogenous, reflexive, or stimulus-driven attention, is attention driven by perceived changes in the environment (Carretié, 2014; Lundwall, 2023). Armed robbers interrupting your intellectual coffee time and making you snap your head toward the kerfuffle would be an example of this type of attention initiation.

The effect can be reliably recreated in the lab with stimuli as simple as pictures or symbols (De Oca & Black, 2013). The physical changes caused by this involuntary attentional shift through the autonomic nervous system can be measured in everything from changes in heart rate, perspiration, or pupil dilation (Öhman, Esteves, Flykt & Soares, 1993; Sokolov, 1963; Spinks & Siddle, 1983).

When the top-down attentional process is interrupted, we drive our foveal vision (see vision chapter) to the stimulus (Carretié, 2014). In support of that redirection of vision, there is an increase in the activity of areas of the brain associated with visual processing (Asplund et al., 2010; Rees, Frith & Lavie, 2001; Hopfinger & Mangun, 2001; Serences & Yantis, 2007).

In the simplest of terms, when something is perceived as a threat to us or is sufficiently emotionally arousing, it can automatically capture our vision and attention without our conscious direction (Fox et al., 2007). Whatever we were doing, likely a top-down task, is either abandoned or our ongoing performance is measurably impaired. Your brain knows what is important now, and it is certain that you need to know. This attentional 'grab' is more indicative of the unexpected close-quarter threat that presents itself to a law enforcement officer. TFS is a method to prepare for and receive training to deploy an appropriate response to a bottom-up attentional event.

Conclusion

It appears that attention can move in the visual field independently of the fixation position.

- Newby & Rock, 1998

Attention and vision are two separate functions. Just because we look at something does not mean we see or pay attention to it. As trainers, we must know and understand these fundamental differences and ensure that our programs of instruction consider them.

Sometimes, vision and attention overlap, leading us to focus on what we observe. At other times, this connection falters. Occasionally, we control what we concentrate on; at other times, we do not. A familiar example of this is reading. If you finish a sentence, paragraph, page, or chapter and think, "I have no idea what I just read," you have encountered this phenomenon. Your vision was directed to the words, and your eyes scanned them dutifully. However, you were not attending to the task; your mind wandered to a more engaging subject, even if that was not your intention.

For maximum training effect from the outset, we need our shooters to be focused beyond their bodies and guns and into their surroundings as soon as possible and as often as possible. The information driving their decision to use force operationally will be externally sourced. Training should be in line with the operational objective from the start.

Attention does not have to be an add-on or an afterthought in training design. If attentional focus is part of the process from the outset, it can run symbiotically with the associated motor skill development. A person learning to draw a handgun effectively can still be training their attentional focus simultaneously. Once the nomenclature of the holster is introduced and some familiarization is complete, there is no need for the shooter to routinely look at the holster during the draw. Part of training on the drawing process should be that vision and attention are directed elsewhere, toward the intended target or the contextually relevant stimuli that prompted the need to access the handgun.

We must consciously pay attention to our targets to train target-focused shooting on inanimate objects like steel, paper, or cardboard. The reality of a lethal force encounter will likely have your amygdala grab hold of your attention and vision and drive both toward the thing that is so terrifying it needs to be shot. During live-fire training, we must be effortfully focused on driving our attention and keeping it focused on what we want to shoot. Building this skill aims to prepare people for the physiological and psychological responses their bodies are likely to initiate in real-world situations.

CHAPTER 8 - SKILL TYPES

For the things we have to learn before we can do them, we learn by doing them.

-   Aristotle

Open and closed skills describe two different formats of learning and training. There is a difference between training for a test and training for your life. Understanding how open and closed skills are defined can provide clarity, making it easier to identify where time and resources are being allocated.

Closed Skills

Closed skills are executed in controlled environments with consistent external factors, such as static shooting drills on a range or driving a vehicle on a closed track. Working on closed skills allows trainees to refine specific techniques in a constant and predictable environment.

Closed skills have an important place early in the learning process. They are specific physical tasks performed in a controlled environment. The performer can focus entirely on executing the skill without adapting to changing conditions. Closed skill training is perfect when forming the foundation of newly introduced technical abilities, partially due to the systematic and specific nature of the training itself and partially due to the controlled environment. The road to automaticity begins here. However, training where external factors remain constant can only be considered a starting point if the goal is a robust and adaptable skill.

Relying solely on closed skills can create a false sense of readiness for the learner and the trainer. Learners might excel in controlled drills but struggle with high-pressure, real-world situations that demand adaptability and decision-making under stress. The hallowed handgun qualification is a textbook example of a closed skill. It may have an administrative use, but does not correlate with operational excellence (Morrison, 1998). Closed skills should be significantly reduced for law enforcement officers as soon as possible. Note that I use the word reduced, not eliminated. Closed skills do not fully capture the complexities and unpredictability of real-life encounters. They do have a place, and live fire range work is an example of important closed skill training that must continue. Whenever people can train, they should, but the range is not the only place to build firearm skills. Open skills should outweigh closed skill processes as training progresses.

Open Skills

In contrast, open skills are performed in dynamic and unpredictable settings, such as a police officer fighting to prevail in a tense, uncertain, or rapidly evolving situation or an officer driving a patrol vehicle to cross a busy city to respond to an emergency. Open skills require quick decision-making and adaptability.

Open skills are essential for responding effectively to rapidly evolving situations, confrontations, or emergencies. Such skills demand quick thinking and adaptability in skill application, as the performer must adjust their actions based on the evolving context. Although our officers rely heavily on open skills in real-world operations, these skills are not proportionately emphasized in their training programs.

Open skills present a greater training challenge because they must be performed in dynamic, unpredictable environments where constantly changing external factors directly impact performance. That can be tough to organize, especially when live ammunition is involved.

Open skills are essential for environments where situational awareness and adaptability are critical. Cultivating open skills is essential for armed professionals, as failure to do so can leave them unprepared for making rapid, high-stakes decisions in unpredictable, high-risk situations. Open skills enable the development of resilience and the ability to adapt to rapidly changing circumstances. Training regimens emphasizing open skills enhance cognitive flexibility and decision-making abilities, better equipping officers for high-pressure, evolving events.

Conclusion

Law enforcement training generally, and firearms training specifically primarily focus on closed skills. This can lead to a false sense of preparedness, sometimes referred to as an illusion of learning. A notable example of this for law enforcement is the handgun qualification.

The state of Florida recently changed its law enforcement handgun qualification, integrating single-step movements for stages ranging from 1 to 7 yards. The failure rate for seasoned officers spiked dramatically. The new test was still very much a closed skill test. The problem was that the officers were so conditioned to pass the old static test that asking them to take a single step was outside their operational competence. It sounds ludicrous, I know - but it is sadly true. Inflexible, rote skills practiced routinely have zero transferability to new tests. Now imagine how ineffective they become when applied to dynamic, real-life situations that demand adaptability and quick thinking.

Effective training for open skills must occur in environments that simulate the complexities of real-world interactions. This includes scenario-based drills and high-fidelity training that challenge people to think critically and make decisions under pressure. Traditional methods that focus solely on closed skills, such as repetitive drills in controlled settings, are insufficient for preparing officers for the unpredictability they will face in the field. However, we do not all have the time and logistical support for large-scale scenario training.

If we must spend time in the closed skill realm because those are the resources we have been allocated, we need to leverage it to the best of our ability and maximize the transferability of the skills we practice. We can shape closed-skill training to drive real-world results by ensuring it supports the skills needed in practical, operational settings. Every drill, task, and concept we invest time into should be purposefully aligned with real-world job demands. If we only do things to stay compliant with the dusty lesson plan written ten years ago or to pass tests, we will not produce high-level performers. Prevailing in real-world operations is built through consistently training hundreds of small skills, reinforced by thousands of high-quality and varied repetitions.

This is where TFS comes in. Incorporating TFS into your training programs provides reality-based context for closed skill development. We know that when we work a closed skill for a rote drill, the stimulus is pre-planned, the target is positioned and identified, and the number of rounds is usually specific and predetermined. Where the shooter looks or what they are paying attention to is not often a priority or even a consideration. It needs to be. The skill of focusing attention externally can be worked on effectively, even in a closed skill realm. Vision and attention aimed outward are paramount to success. If vision and attention are trained any other way, it creates an additional adjustment the shooter must make under pressure, hindering their ability to transfer skills effectively to real-world situations. Just like an officer who has never trained to move their feet before, during, or after the shooting and then finds it overwhelming to do so - the same potential fate awaits the officers who now need to be focused outward but end up staring at their gun instead (Vickers & Lewinski, 2012) because that is how they practiced on the range.

CHAPTER 9 - WHERE & WHEN IS

THE TECHNIQUE RELEVANT

Many shooters at less than 5 yards indicated they did not see the red dot. They used a "point shooting" / kinesthetic method.

- NLEFIA OIS National Survey, 2019 - 2024

If I were to provide a transferable definition of where the TFS technique is applicable, I would say that it is when the target you need to shoot is large, close, and unobstructed. For example, an adult male 8 feet away with no one else between you and him would fit this definition. An adult male 45 feet away, holding a hostage in front of his body, offering only a partial view of his head, would not. As I said very early on, anyone who claims that sights are always required is wrong; anyone who tells you sights are never required is equally wrong. There is a time and a place for pure TFS with no visual reference to the gun. There is also a time and place for using the sighting system, although I would still advocate for remaining target-focused when using sights whenever possible (see TFS and Iron Sights).

As for when, if they're close enough that you can smell their breath and they need to be shot, I think you have your answer.

Building Search - My Ah-Ha Moment

This is a good point to reflect on how I came to learn about the TFS technique. My journey into the realm of TFS is part of the reason I am an advocate. It was a journey of necessity, and by telling you the story of how I stumbled into using it, I hope to tie together the concepts shared thus far in the book.

I first discovered the technique during my initiation into building search/room clearance training about fifteen years ago. I use the word 'discover' specifically referring to my personal realization. I am under no illusion that I discovered anything that was not already well established and recorded - see the history chapter. I just had no idea about TFS; I had never even considered the idea. I had learned to use my pistol and carbine the old school way with iron sights, usually with one eye closed/squinted and a perpetual front sight focus. It served me well for my closed skill of shooting targets on a range and passing the preliminary shooting tests to advance into tactical training.

My training quickly progressed from the closed skill of the flat range to an introduction to searching buildings. Building search training felt intense for me and the others on my course. It was a steep step up from the range, and we moved around and in front of each other with guns for the first time. It is easy to forget what a huge change in difficulty and responsibility that is after experiencing nothing but the rigidity of the learning environment on the range. This is the type of training realm where bonds of trust are forged on a team.

Once we had mastered the dance steps on how to move safely following our team's tactics, the complexity was increased. The training was shifting from closed skills to open skills more and more as each day passed. Paper targets were added to the rooms we were searching, then those were intermixed with photo-realistic decision targets, and then we had role players added. It was a fast progression, and at the time I did not fully appreciate how good the training was. I had no benchmark against which to measure it. It was all I knew, so to me, it was normal.

I noticed that, when I shot, I began to look beyond my gun much more frequently. It was happening instinctively, and I am unsure how long I was doing it before I noticed it. Where I was going and my teammates' positions forced my attention to be external and broad. I was no longer looking for my sights when I had a target identified. My sights were less important than the information I needed from a narrow external focus of attention to decide when or if to shoot. The simple binary decision-making associated with a target turning on the range was no longer applicable. Now I needed to THINK, not just stare at my front sight and shoot. Now I needed my vision and my attention focused on the area ahead of me. I needed to use that acquired information to make my shooting decisions.

The need for processing speed increased as our pace of movement increased, the targets got closer, and the decisions and responses became more demanding. I often couldn't remember using my sights after an engagement. I found myself wondering if I had forgotten I used them due to so much happening, or if I had just not used them at all. I still remember the first time I took shots intending to be TFS. I pushed through an open door, took a sharp left turn to clear a narrow alcove behind that door, and saw my target. This was a paper/photo style target. I scanned visually for cues as I brought the gun up and issued a verbal challenge. I could see that I had a 'shoot' target, and I clustered a group of shots into the chest. My visual focus remained on the target throughout the process. I watched the shots appear one after the other without using or referencing my sights. That is when my close quarter shooting technique was forever changed.

Whenever my target was large, close, and unobstructed, I used TFS. I used it in all aspects of training. Live fire and Simmunition™. I used it on paper, cardboard, steel, and live role players. I used it during vehicle stops, pedestrian stops, and heavily during building searches. I felt like I had unlocked a secret code. My decision-making was on point because I was looking at the subject and perpetually seeking information. My confidence grew in the technique, and I was making faster decisions and quicker, more accurate shot placements than my peers who were sticking with tradition. I was not blindly captivated by the idea. When I had to make a shot down a long hallway, across a street, or into a subject obscured by a hostage, I still locked onto that front sight for all I was worth. Even as an experimenter, I knew there was a time and place for this, as it also had limitations.

I came to understand this process (technique) through personal exploration, reflection, and discovery. What I instinctively wanted to do was already well established as a battle-tested, proven aiming technique. I had no idea about that history, I did not know what I did not know. The years of research that followed were a means by which I sought to understand what I was doing and how I was doing it. The way I wanted to use vision and attention to hone speed and decision-making felt natural, and it aligned with what I later learned about top-down and bottom-up attention. I learned that the speed I gained by not trying to change my visual focus from the target to the sighting system was buying me the fractions of a second I needed to succeed. Knowing when I could ignore visual irrelevancies in my environment, including my gun, and filter my attention to what is important now, enhanced the quality of my decisions.

Some authors have tried to measure the distance between when and where TFS works in feet and yards. Though that can be accurate in a closed skill realm, it is not possible to determine an absolute distance in a dynamic, evolving, high-consequence event. The risk of throwing out a number is that it becomes misinterpreted dogma, like the often and brutally misrepresented "21-foot rule", which was never a rule (Tueller, 1983).

When deciding how to aim a gun, whether sighted or unsighted, context must drive the decision. Personal levels of skill and confidence also play into the process. As Inspector Harry Callahan once said, *"A man's got to know his limitations"*, or if you prefer gender neutral Greek philosophy over iconic 1970s movie cops, *"Know thyself"*. Just as no one can tell you when to shoot, no one can dictate precisely how you should aim or at what distance.

Distance is Relative

Distance is relative; it is also ambiguous and complex when people try to use it as a metric. Although I have previously stipulated and stand by the opinion that distance alone cannot be a measure to endorse a technique, distance is certainly a dominant factor. The closer an officer is to their subject, the more danger they are in. When gunfire is being exchanged, classic range marksmanship is irrelevant - the will to win and do so fast is far more influential on the outcome. People with no training in handgun use present a formidable threat at close distance (Lewinski et al., 2015).

The following reference material offers an opportunity to compare a high-level overview of areas where the TFS technique has been previously endorsed and where officer-involved shootings (OIS) occur. Though there are many variables beyond distance, it is an interesting place to start. The first stop on this journey is with some of the authors from Chapter 2. Many of the writers set a limit on the distance at which unsighted handgun use became ineffective. Their findings are summarized in the following table (see Figure 13).

Author	Endorsed TFS out to...
Bill Cassidy	25 feet
William Fairbairn	30 feet
Robert Taubert	30 feet
Chuck Klein	30 feet
Charles Askins Jr	36 feet
Bill Jordan	45 feet
Rex Applegate	50 feet

Figure 13 *List of TFS authors and their defined maximum distance for use of TFS*

I would be more reserved than most of those authors in distance, even in a closed skill realm. Let us look at some OIS data and compare it to their distances. It is critical to note that this data is incomplete, to say the least. OIS in the U.S.A. is statistically a very low-occurring event compared to the number of police interactions with the public (Bozeman et al., 2018), contrary to the media-driven perception. In addition to the event's rarity, the data recording is inconsistent. There is no uniform requirement to record this data, nor to share it. Accepting those limitations, the following data is certainly interesting but will always be incomplete.

The Data-Driven Danger Zones

2019 National Policing Institute Data

In 2019, the National Policing Institute (NPI) published OIS data from a large sample size. They initially looked at high-level data provided by the Major City Chiefs Association over a ten-year period from 2005 to 2015. Following that analysis, they embarked on a partnership with the National Police Foundation in 2015. They acquired a large data sample with more specific details from 2015 to 2017, involving more than 1,000 incidents. One of the metrics measured was the distance between the subject and the officer when the first round was fired, shown in Figure 14.

Initially, it looks like the final column 36+ is the biggest area. The data presentation is somewhat misleading because the final column is measured differently from the others. The first seven columns each show the number of incidents that occurred within a window of five feet. The final column is essentially infinite. It covers everything that happened beyond 36 feet.

Distance between officer and the subject when the first round was fired
(measured in feet)

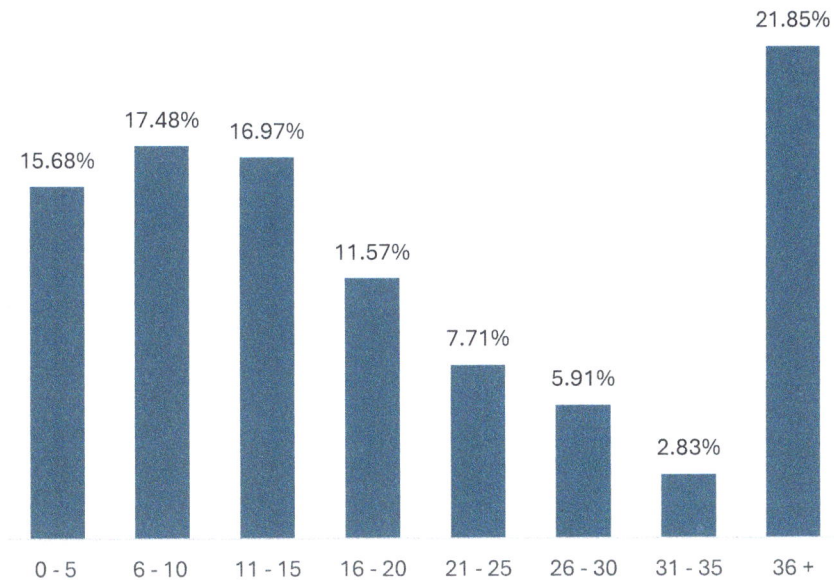

Figure 14 Distance between officer and subject when first round was fired. 2019 NPI Data

That initial oddity aside, let us look at this data through the lens of the historic TFS advocates. Even if we applied the most conservative opinion of 25 feet from Bill Cassidy, that would still account for nearly 70% of incidents. Taking everything that happened from 0 – 25 feet and putting it into one column is shown in Figure 15.

Distance between officer and the subject when the first round was fired
(measured in feet)

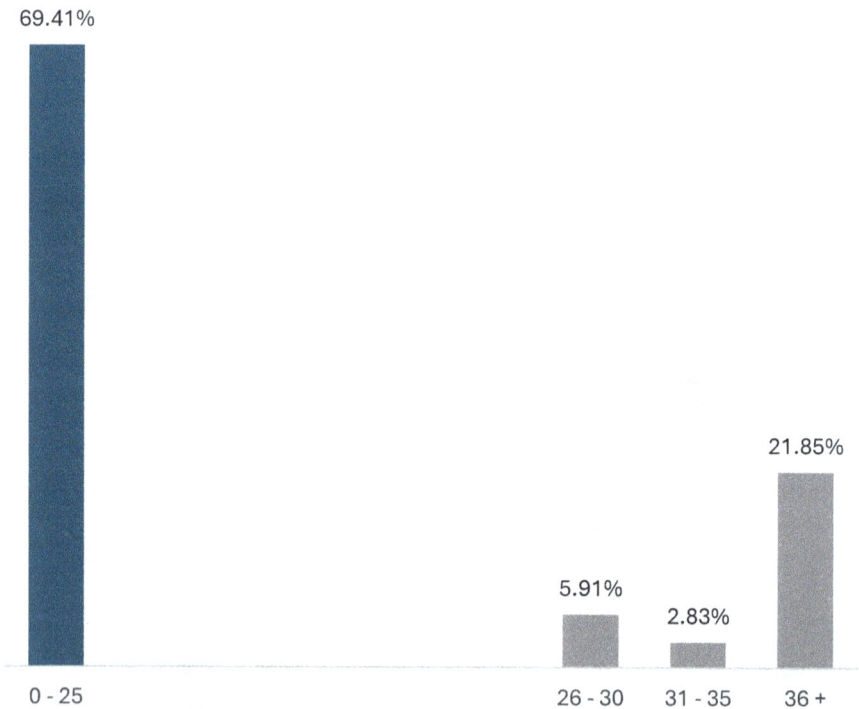

Figure 15 Distance between officer and subject when first round was fired. The first five columns have been consolidated to display 0–25 feet as a single data point. 2019 NPI Data

The majority of the TFS authors capped their non-sighted aiming at 30 feet. That would break down the NPI data as shown in Figure 16. Looking at this data within the parameters set by most of the TFS authors, the technique appears to be the appropriate aiming solution for three-quarters of the incidents documented.

Distance between officer and the subject when the first round was fired
(measured in feet)

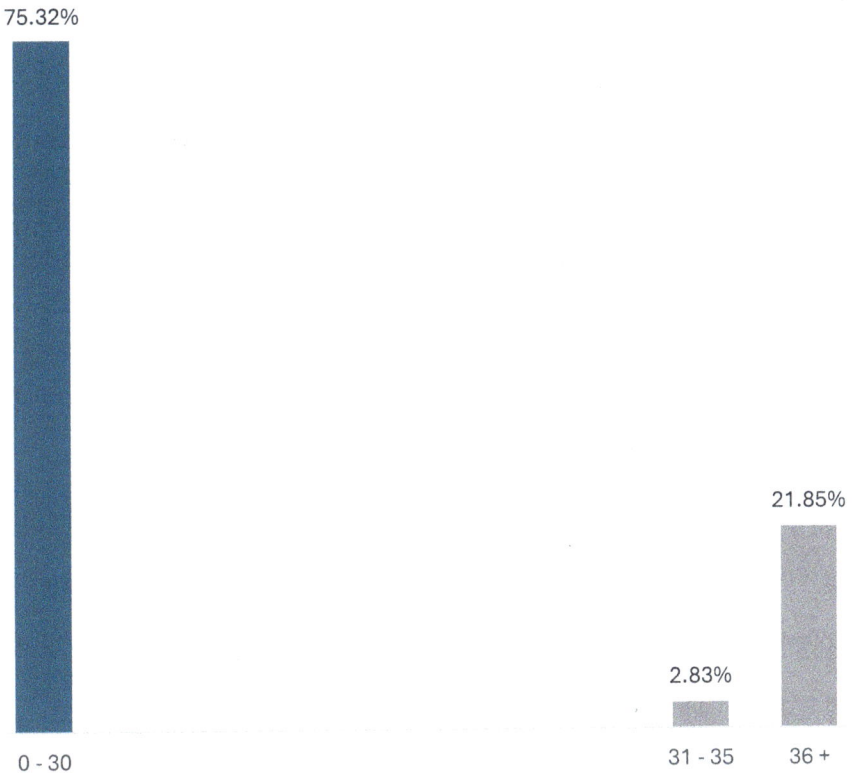

Figure 16 Distance between officer and subject when first round was fired. The first six columns have been consolidated to display 0–30 feet as a single data point. 2019 NPI Data

Law Enforcement Officers Killed and Assaulted 1987 – 2023

The data-rich set that the FBI collates in the Law Enforcement Officers Killed and Assaulted (LEOKA) is vast. As with all things data-related in this realm, there are also limitations. Participation is voluntary, so it does not include incidents from every agency in the country. In addition to the fragmented participation, the data is also skewed regarding the result of the incident. LEOKA only offers OIS data from incidents where officers were killed. If there was an OIS where the officer prevailed (always the goal), that data would not be captured in LEOKA. The shooting data does not include injury; we only see stats from events where the officers were killed, so we cannot say this data is a complete representation of where all OISs occur.

Considering the limitations of these statistics, the data can still be very useful. The volume of information is huge, but more importantly, the information is also very consistent. Year after year, there is consistency in the distance where officers are being killed. Decade after decade, there is consistency in the fact that firearms are the weapon causing the most deaths. The charts in the following tables are from data recorded from 1987 to 2023. As a brief summary of the data in its complete format, it breaks down like this:

- 2,372 Officers were feloniously killed
- 2,159 Officers were killed with a firearm (91%)

Of those 2,159 Officers killed with a firearm, the distance from their killer was reported in 1,754 instances. The other 405 incidents did not have a known or reported distance. Figure 17 shows the distance between the officer and the subject in those 1,754 events.

Distance between officer and subject LEOKA 1987 -2023
(measured in feet)

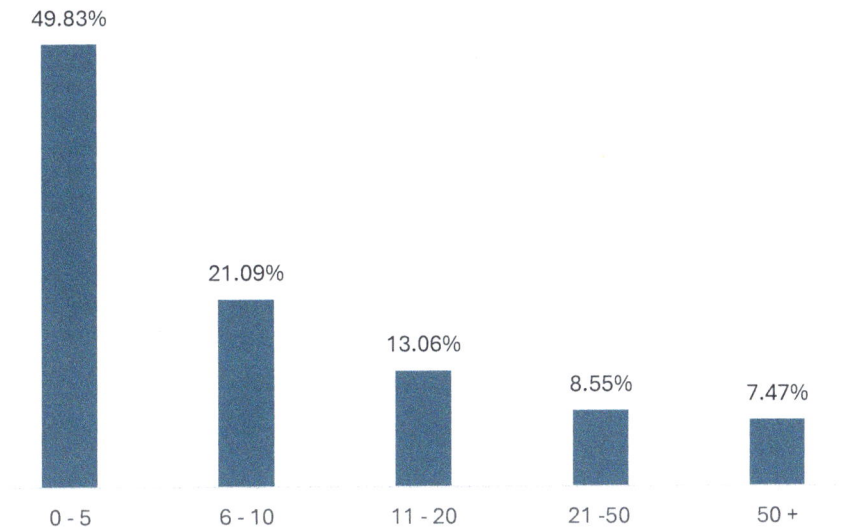

Figure 17 *Distance between the officer and the subject when the officer was shot and killed. LEOKA 1987 -2023*

The initial data is striking. Despite the potentially infinite distance, the smallest column is the 50+ feet column. There is an incredible consistency in correlation between proximity and the number of deaths. There could be a host of reasons why proximity is so closely related to fatality. Here are a few likely possibilities - It could be that most law enforcement interactions happen at conversational distance, so that is where the most violence has the potential to occur. Traffic stops are notoriously unpredictable encounters that can have deadly outcomes; they are another example of a common law enforcement interaction that occurs at conversational distance. The higher deaths from gunfire in proximity could be accuracy-related – we know that novices can be accurate when they are close. That is certainly supported by the research about the accuracy of naive shooters (Lewinski et al., 2015). The further away the officer can get, the less likely the shooter is to be able to hit them. It could be some of those reasons, or perhaps others. Whatever the reason, the fact remains that more officers are killed by gunfire within 5 feet of their assailant than at any other distance.

The breakdown from LEOKA does not come in as many increments as the NPI study, making it harder to correlate with the maximal limits of the TFS authors' boundaries. I cannot legitimately slice it up to a 25-foot chart or a 30-foot chart. Even with that restriction, by clustering the first three increments together as one data set and showing how many officers were shot and killed within 20 feet, it very sadly, very quickly becomes a dominant percentage at 83.98% (see Figure 18).

In terms of the number of people who gave their lives within that distance in service of others, it is a heart-wrenching one thousand four hundred and seventy-three officers. Twenty feet and closer is a dangerous place to be. Speed matters, movement matters. If the opportunity is available to return fire, TFS is critical at this distance.

Distance between officer and subject LEOKA 1987 -2023
(measured in feet)

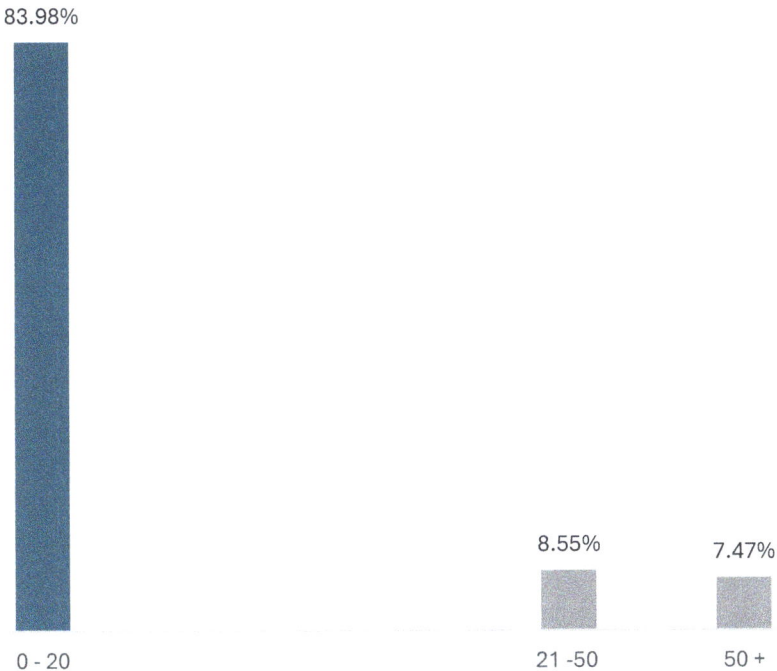

Figure 18 Distance between the officer and the subject when the officer was shot and killed. The first three columns have been consolidated to display 0–20 feet as a single data point. LEOKA 1987 -2023

MILO Study

The final data set is from a recent unpublished study completed by a law enforcement researcher working for MILO. MILO is a world-leading provider of interactive simulation training, curriculum, range design, and equipment. This data was presented during a law enforcement instructor development conference in March of 2025. Two hundred and fifty videos of officer-involved shootings from across the country were broken down into varying data points for the project. One of the data sets was the distance between the officer and the subject when the incident began (see Figure 19). The increments used to display the data are slightly different than the previous two studies. The first increment was termed contact distance - defined as being within an arm's length or less.

By combining the first two criteria to represent a range of 0–6 feet, the percentage is 52% (see Figure 20), which closely matches the LEOKA data set of 0–5 feet, shown at 49.83% (see Figure 17).

Distance between officer and the subject when the first round was fired
(measured in feet)

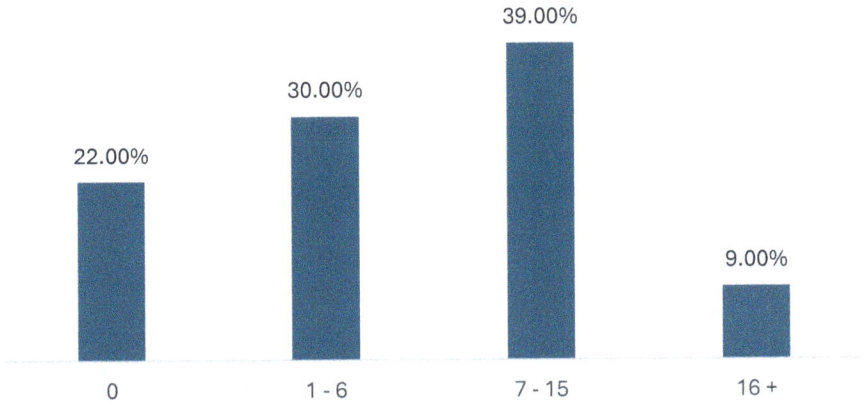

Figure 19 Distance between the officer and the subject when the first round was fired. MILO 2025.

Distance between officer and the subject when the first round was fired
(measured in feet)

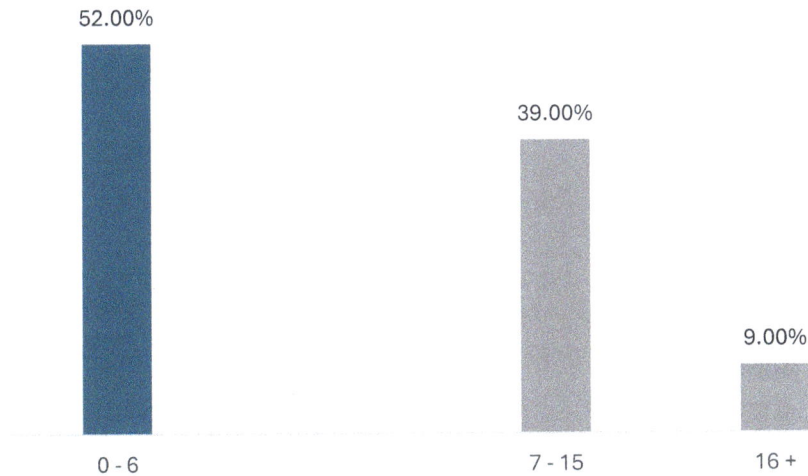

Figure 20 Distance between the officer and the subject when the first round was fired. The first two columns have been consolidated to display 0–6 feet as a single data point. MILO 2025

Taking it one stage further and looking at all the data from 0-15 feet in one bundle makes for a dramatic comparison (see Figure 21). More than 90% of these incidents began with the officer and subject within 15 feet of one another. Every one of the TFS authors would comfortably put 15 feet or closer as a viable distance for the technique. This would mean that more than 90% of the incidents in this study could have met the criteria for a TFS-initiated response based on proximity.

Distance between officer and the subject when the first round was fired
(measured in feet)

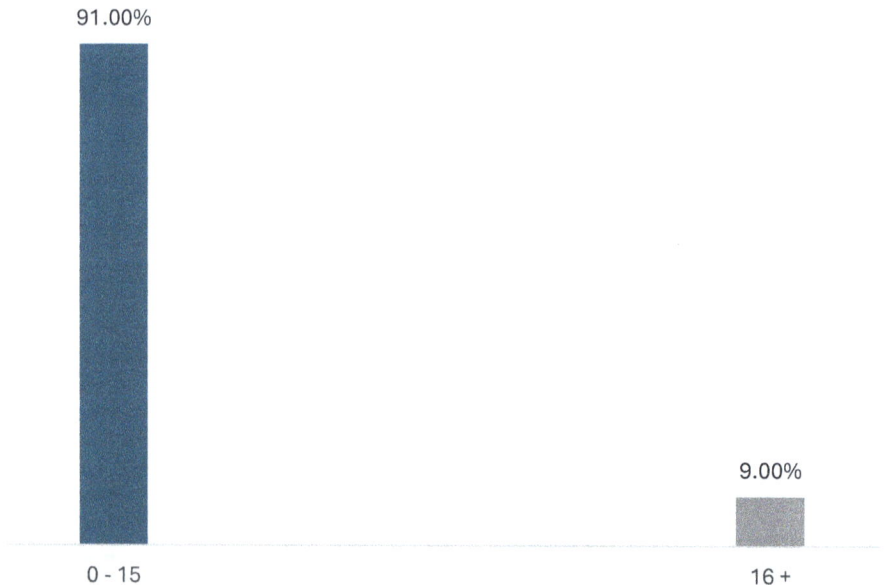

Figure 21 *Distance between the officer and the subject when the first round was fired. The first three columns have been consolidated to display 0–15 feet as a single data point. MILO 2025*

Conclusion

The technique is relevant when the nature of the violence is close; tense, uncertain, and rapidly evolving - as the Supreme Court would say (*Graham v. Connor,* 1989). When the target that needs to be shot is large, close, and unobstructed, sights may be the last thing you either need or can find. In those circumstances, when fractions of a second count and you can smell the bad breath of your would-be murderer – I'd assert that target-focused decision-making and shooting is the correct answer to the unwelcome puzzle you have been called upon to solve.

CHAPTER 10 – EVIDENCE
INFORMED LEARNING

Growth and comfort are incompatible.

- Don Alwes

This fundamental truth about human development applies directly to firearms training. The comfortable, traditional methods that feel easy and intuitive often impede the robust learning officers need for operational effectiveness.

Evidence-Based Learning Principles for Firearms Instruction

Law enforcement firearms training has long been influenced by educational myths and well-intentioned but scientifically unsupported theories. From the persistent belief in learning styles to block training and test-based approaches to course design. These misconceptions can seriously undermine the effectiveness of practical training and even compromise officer safety. This chapter examines the research that informs us about how adults learn and retain motor skills most effectively, with specific applications to firearms instruction. This will help lay the foundation for the coming chapter on training TFS skills for aiming.

The true stakes of firearms training aren't measured in hitting targets, but in lives protected and tragedies averted. Officers must be prepared to make accurate, rapid decisions about the use of force while managing multiple stressors and task demands. Traditional training methods, often based on intuition rather than research, fail to adequately prepare officers for these complex demands. By grounding training in an evidence informed approach, we can build more effective programs that enhance robust skill transferability and increase both officer and public safety.

Effective firearms instruction requires understanding how we acquire, consolidate, store, and recall motor skills under varying conditions of stress and complexity. The principles outlined in this chapter are grounded in decades of research from cognitive psychology, motor learning, and education. This will provide firearms instructors with a foundational guide for evidence-based strategies to maximize skill retention, promote transfer to real-world scenarios, and build the robust capabilities officers need in dynamic situations. I encourage digging deeper into all the associated references that spark your interest. This chapter represents a high-level overview and serves as a mere peek into the perpetual learning possibilities.

The Learning Styles Myth

One of the most pervasive myths in law enforcement training is the belief in learning styles, particularly the VARK model (Visual, Auditory, Reading/Writing, Kinesthetic). Despite widespread popularity, this theory lacks scientific support and hinders effective training design and delivery.

The most comprehensive review of learning styles research was conducted by Pashler et al. (2008), who examined hundreds of studies and concluded that the contrast between the enormous popularity of learning styles and the lack of credible evidence is "striking and disturbing". Their analysis found no adequate evidence that matching instructional methods to supposed learning preferences improves outcomes.

Subsequent research has consistently reinforced these findings. Willingham et al. (2015) found no evidence supporting the claim that people learn better when information is presented in their preferred style. More recently, Aslaksen and Lorås (2018) examined learning styles specifically in motor skill acquisition and demonstrated that supposed learning style preferences had no impact on motor learning outcomes.

Why The Myths Persist

Learning styles theory persists for three main reasons. First, it has intuitive appeal—most people can identify with one of the proposed styles. Second, it provides a simple explanation for training difficulties, allowing instructors to attribute poor performance to "mismatched learning styles" rather than examining the effectiveness of their instruction. Third, the learning styles industry has created extensive commercial materials and training programs that perpetuate the myth despite the availability of discrediting scientific evidence. This futile fascination diverts attention from evidence-based methods that could significantly improve training outcomes (Rohrer & Pashler, 2012).

Having examined what doesn't work in training design, we can now focus on what does. The following principles provide the foundation for effective firearms instruction. Unlike the intuitive appeal of learning styles, these evidence-based approaches may initially feel counterintuitive but consistently produce superior long-lasting results.

Evidence-Informed Principles of Adult Motor Learning

Understanding how adults acquire motor skills provides an evidence-informed foundation for effective firearms instruction. Decades of motor learning research have revealed several key principles essential to the development of shooting skills. This is particularly relevant for perception-action capabilities, such as TFS, which require integrating multiple sensory systems and adapting to varied real-world conditions.

Learning vs. Performance

A critical distinction in firearms training is between learning and performance. Schmidt and Lee (2019) emphasize that performance during practice does not always reflect learning, as various temporary factors can influence immediate performance while having little impact on long-term skill retention.

Performance: The demonstration of skills or knowledge during instruction or practice, often with guidance, prompts, or immediate feedback present.

Learning: The retention and independent application of skills or knowledge in varied contexts without immediate instruction or prompts, demonstrable on demand, after a delay from initial training.

An officer might perform well during range practice due to optimal conditions and instructor guidance. The same officer may struggle in dynamic scenarios if their training has prioritized temporary performance over enduring learning. Conversely, challenging practice conditions may initially impair performance, but they can also develop more robust, transferable skills that emerge over time.

The Training Implication

Effective firearms training should focus on learning rather than just performance. This means trainers must understand that although practice conditions with appropriate challenge and variation might temporarily lower short-term (initial) performance, they are crucial for developing lasting skills and real-world readiness – far more valuable than the limited benefits of repetitive, simplified drills. There are several principles trainers can follow to ensure they choose an appropriate time to measure learning, how to measure learning most effectively, and some red flags to look out for where performance and learning may be misinterpreted.

When to Measure Learning:

- Wait at least 24-48 hours after initial instruction to assess retention
- For complex motor skills, reassess at 1-week and 1-month intervals
- Schedule unannounced assessments to prevent 'cramming' or recent practice effects
- Harness opportunities where fatigue or stress are naturally occurring – assess what they can do at the end of a long shift, or work week (skill on demand in sub-optimal conditions is a strong indicator of learning over performance)

How to Measure Learning:

- Change assessment conditions from training conditions (lighting, positions, targets, time constraints, and induce malfunctions)
- Remove instructor cues and coaching during an assessment
- Require students to explain 'why' they are doing what they are doing
- Test under mild stress or distraction (within safety parameters)
- Use scenario-based assessments that require decision-making plus skill execution

Red Flags (Performance, Not Learning):

- Performance degrades significantly when conditions change slightly
- The student needs verbal reminders for basic safety protocols
- Students cannot explain the reasons behind their actions
- Skills deteriorate rapidly without regular instructor guidance
- Performance stalls or deteriorates when required to combine motor skills and cognitive load (decision-making, identifying threats, utilizing cover)

The Three Stages of Motor Learning

Fitts and Posner's (1967) three-stage model remains fundamental to understanding skill acquisition and provides crucial guidance for adapting instruction as learners progress. Each stage is characterized by different learning mechanisms, error patterns, and instructional needs that must be recognized and addressed appropriately. Despite being established years ago, the stages still provide a clear and practical roadmap for coaches to identify and guide skill progression. As you read each descriptive stage, I encourage you to consider a student's learning journey and advancement. Note how the feedback frequency and content change throughout each stage. Feedback will be explored in more detail next.

Cognitive Stage

During this initial phase, learners require explicit instruction and frequent feedback as they develop a fundamental understanding of the skill requirements. Performance is highly variable and heavily dependent on conscious attention. For TFS, officers in the cognitive stage are learning the fundamental principles behind aiming with their bodies, establishing basic motor patterns, and understanding how various sensory inputs can provide feedback for technique efficacy.

Instructors working with cognitive-stage learners should clearly explain underlying principles, demonstrate the desired technique clearly, and offer frequent, specific feedback about successful and unsuccessful attempts. This is also a place to start showing learners where and how to source feedback from their own performance. Officers must understand what to do, why specific techniques are effective, and how to recognize correct execution. This conceptual foundation, along with the development of basic motor skills, is essential for progressing to more advanced stages of learning and performance.

Associative Stage

As motor skills become more consistent, learners can detect and correct many errors themselves. Performance becomes less variable, and the cognitive demands of skill execution decrease. Officers in the associative stage are refining their shooting technique, developing internal feedback mechanisms, and adapting their skills to varied conditions.

Instruction during the associative stage should emphasize self-evaluation and error correction. Officers should be encouraged to analyze their performance, identify improvement areas, and experiment with technique modifications. Feedback frequency can be reduced as officers develop internal standards for performance evaluation. In sync with this reduction in feedback from the coach, the learner should be increasing their ability to self-assess their performance. Practice conditions should introduce variability to promote adaptability and prevent the development of overly rigid movement patterns.

Autonomous Stage

Skills become automatic and resistant to interference from other task demands or environmental stressors. Officers can execute techniques reliably under stress with minimal cognitive load, directing attention toward decision-making and environmental considerations rather than basic skill execution.

Training for autonomous-stage performers should focus on maintaining skills under challenging conditions and integrating TFS with all other capabilities. Practice should include high-fidelity scenarios, time pressure, and competing task demands that closely replicate the pressures and complexity of real-world operations. Feedback should be minimal and focused on fine-tuning rather than basic skill correction.

Three Stages of Motor Learning

Figure 22 *A graded image showing the crossover in stages of motor learning from cognitive, to associative, to autonomous*

Understanding these stages helps instructors adjust their approach appropriately and set realistic expectations for skill development. Rushing officers through these stages or applying inappropriate instructional methods for a given stage can impair learning and delay skill development. Although there are three distinct phases, consider this a sliding scale rather than three distinctly different boxes.

The divisions between defined stages cross and blur together as a learner transitions from one to another (see Figure 22). Knowing where individuals are on the scale will help define how we engage students with tasks and feedback. Knowing where learners are in their skill development journey is crucial for practical training. The type and amount of feedback offered should directly correlate to which part of their learning journey they are on.

Understanding these stages helps instructors distinguish between temporary performance improvements and genuine learning progression. Officers may show impressive performance gains during instruction that do not represent stable learning if the foundational cognitive and associative work has not been completed.

Recognizing where learners are in their skill development journey is imperative because it directly influences how we should provide feedback. The type, timing, and focus of feedback must align with the learner's stage to maximize effectiveness.

Feedback

Feedback is a critical part of the motor skills training process. It involves learners gaining information regarding their performance, which aids in skill acquisition, refinement, and overall improvement. Misconceptions about feedback often lead to challenges, such as the tendency to view it solely as a corrective tool, which can inhibit a learner's motivation and self-efficacy. Recognizing the complexities of feedback and its role is key to maximizing learners' potential for developing robust, effective skills.

Types of Feedback

Feedback can be broadly placed into two categories: intrinsic and extrinsic feedback. Intrinsic feedback arises from the performer's own sensory experiences. Extrinsic feedback on performance is from external sources.

Intrinsic Feedback

Intrinsic feedback may also be inherent (Schmidt et al., 2019). It is internally generated from the performer of a motor skill, in our case, the shooter. This feedback can be anything sensory, from seeing shot placement on a target to feeling some element of their movement process. Intrinsic feedback is vital for self-regulation and skill refinement, especially as performers become more experienced. The better a shooter understands their performance and what success looks and feels like, the more efficiently they can hone their skills.

Extrinsic Feedback

Extrinsic feedback refers to externally sourced information provided to shooters during or after a performance or practice session. This type of feedback can take many forms, most commonly verbal cues from coaches, but it can also be visual demonstrations or video analyses. Extrinsic feedback's timing, frequency, and presentation can significantly influence motivation and learning outcomes. In the early stages of skill acquisition, extrinsic feedback is critical. The shooter may not know what constitutes success and what is 'right'. Helping them become more aware of how they contribute to self-improvement is essential. For novices, that structure is likely to come from external sources.

Two other sub-classifications come within the extrinsic realm. The feedback provided can be defined as knowledge of performance or knowledge of results.

Knowledge of Performance

Knowledge of performance (KP) regarding shooting skills is anything observable in the shooter's use of their body or movement. For example, if their draw was inefficient and had extraneous movement, their coach's feedback would meet the definition of KP.

Knowledge of Results

Knowledge of results (KR) can be straightforward and somewhat binary for simple shooting tasks. Results regarding shooting on a range could be as simple as hits or misses, but it could also be the KR concerning a time standard, an overall score, or a ranking. KR could be more complex in an open skill environment. If the task undertaken in training was based on team movement, decision-making, communication, and some form of dynamic skills application, the KR could be far more in-depth. This would be especially apparent if the results were linked to several events. For example, an inadequate perimeter on a building that allowed a subject to escape containment, leading to a pursuit and a challenging and complex use of force, would be a far more in-depth KR than failing to meet an arbitrary range time standard.

Type and Timing of Feedback

Dr. Joan Vickers provides several different classifications of feedback (2007, p. 197), seven of which are shown here. Each of these has a role in coaching motor skills. Part of the art of coaching is knowing where to apply these, although some research can also help with that differentiation. If you only provide feedback in one way and at one time, you are likely not tailoring it to the adaptive needs of your people relative to their current stage on their learning journey.

- **Corrective feedback** refers to technical, tactical, and other task-specific information provided to improve performance

- **Summative feedback** is a form of corrective feedback that is given only after several attempts have been made. In summative feedback, the coach tries to sum up what occurred in terms of major technical, tactical, or other cues

- **Frequency of feedback** refers to how often feedback is provided to an individual or a group within a specific period

- **Instantaneous feedback** is a form of corrective feedback that is given immediately, before people have time to think about their performance

- **Delayed feedback** is a form of corrective feedback provided after a delay so that people have time to think about their performance

- **Faded feedback** occurs when a high frequency of feedback is given early on and then gradually reduced as skill level develops

- **Bandwidth feedback** incorporates a number of the previous characteristics (reduced frequency, delay, fading) into one comprehensive approach to providing feedback as skill level develops

High-frequency instantaneous feedback can have a powerful impact on immediate performance but may hinder long-term learning. As established earlier, our goal must be durable learning rather than impressive practice sessions. More than sixty years ago, research demonstrated that high-frequency feedback creates dependency—when removed, performance drops below that of groups receiving less feedback (Lavery, 1962). If new students constantly receive high volumes of feedback, they can become overly reliant on it.

When high volume feedback is withdrawn and people are required to perform without guidance, the illusion of learning is uncovered as their apparent skills vanish. On the firearms range, that looks like the new shooter who snaps their head around to look for their coach after every course of fire. That is also often the student whose performance only holds up when being coached. When they are left to function alone or take a test, they cannot perform, and the illusion of learning comes crashing down.

A slight delay in feedback can be beneficial if it allows learners to process their performance and reflect on their errors before receiving guidance. This reflective period can enhance the learner's understanding of the skill and improve knowledge retention and transfer. The delay can be anything from a few seconds to a few minutes. Barring some safety issue or a catastrophic failure, there is usually no need to talk to a shooter while they are shooting. They probably can't hear you anyway. They shouldn't be thinking about you, but it stuns me nonetheless how many firearms instructors continue to speak while people are trying to shoot.

The inexplicable need to speak while someone is shooting, or before the handgun has even made it back to the holster, is an epidemic among firearms instructors. I offer you W.A.I.T. as a reminder that your wisdom is better held until your student is ready and able to hear it. W.A.I.T. also serves as a filter between your brain and your mouth. Ask yourself, before you start to speak:

Why

Am

I

Talking

It can be a powerful question to help ensure the words you do choose to use are worthy of being said.

Although feedback can be crucial in the early stages of learning, it should not be perpetually high in volume. Fading feedback is advantageous as skills improve (Swinnen et al., 1990; Winstein & Schmidt, 1990), allowing the performer to become more self-sufficient and self-aware, promoting long-term retention and transfer (Wulf & Shea, 2004).

Bandwidth feedback aligns very well with Fitts and Posner's three-stage model. The observable progress in a shooter's ability and autonomy should result in a reduction of extrinsic feedback. Feedback should gradually fade, allowing shooters to diagnose and correct errors with little external input. For a high-level performer deep in the associative or autonomous stage, feedback is far more likely to be regarding the refinement of a process as opposed to the teaching of an entirely new concept.

The Focus of Feedback, Internal Or External?

As referenced in chapter 7, attention can be broadly categorized as internal or externally focused. The focus of attention can be influenced heavily by the verbiage chosen during feedback. Although this can seem like a small or trivial element, how attention is directed because of feedback can make a big difference to skill development. When it comes to motor skills, an internal focus of attention is a concentration on body movements, such as the movement of the trigger finger. An external focus of attention is directed to the effect of the movement – where they want the bullet to go (Schmidt et al., 2019).

Law enforcement motor skills training receives limited attention and support from scientific research communities. So, we often must look to the sporting realm for the data. The following examples are varied, but they all involve the difference in verbal feedback for a motor skill and the advantage of keeping the learner externally focused during practice.

Novice rowers who were being coached on how to move the oars received different guidance. The externally focused feedback group was told to keep the blade level, while the internally focused feedback group was told to keep your hands level. The external group improved significantly across multiple metrics (Parr & Button, 2009). Externally focused feedback has shown improvement in motor movement in everything from gymnastics (Abdollahipour et al., 2015) to golf (Christina & Alpenfels, 2014).

An experiment measuring balance showed equally distinguishable feedback-oriented results, too. The internal-focused feedback group was told to keep their feet level, while the externally focused group was told to keep the board they were standing on level. Once again, the external nature of the feedback produced higher-level performers (Wulf et al., 1998).

In targeting sports, directing attention externally is also shown to produce superior results. In basketball, instead of feedback encouraging attention to the players' hands, they were directed to focus on the rim. This resulted in a measurable increase in accuracy (Zachry et al., 2005). The same powerful results were replicated in the throwing of darts. Accuracy improved when the players focused on the dart's trajectory and not their hands. In addition to improved accuracy, an external focus of attention led to increased speed and improved economy of motion (Lohse et al., 2010).

Tying this back to firearms instruction, here are a few external ideas for feedback and guidance to get you started:

- Rather than discuss what the trigger finger should do when firing, focus on keeping the gun stable
- Instead of addressing where their feet and hips are positioned, emphasize keeping the target squarely in front of them
- Rather than explain how they place their feet while walking, highlight the importance of maintaining the stability of the gun

Feedback is a Two-Way Street

Effective feedback in firearms training extends beyond the traditional model of instructor-to-student information transfer. The most impactful feedback emerges from a collaborative dialogue where the coach and the shooter actively participate in the learning process. Rather than simply telling a shooter what went wrong, skilled coaches engage their students through thoughtful questioning: "Why did that shot go here?" or "Tell me what happened to your gun during that string of fire?" This approach transforms feedback from a passive reception of information into an active exploration of performance, allowing shooters to develop their intrinsic awareness. At the same time, coaches gain valuable insight into their students' thought processes and perceptual abilities.

The goal of feedback should be to cultivate self-reliant performers who can accurately assess their performance and make appropriate adjustments. By fostering this reciprocal communication, coaches enhance immediate skill development and build the foundation for long-term autonomous performance. When shooters become active participants in their feedback process, they develop the critical thinking skills necessary to diagnose and correct errors independently—a capability that proves invaluable when external guidance is unavailable and peak performance is demanded.

Desirable Difficulty

The principles we've discussed so far—understanding learning stages and providing appropriate feedback—set the foundation for one of the most powerful concepts in motor learning: desirable difficulty. This principle challenges our natural instincts about effective training. Imagine telling officers that to improve their shooting, they need to practice under conditions that will initially make them perform worse. This counterintuitive approach—called desirable difficulty—is one of the most powerful principles in motor learning.

Desirable difficulties are practice conditions that appear to make learning harder but enhance long-term retention and transferability. Developed by Bjork (1994), this principle suggests that learning is enhanced when practice conditions introduce appropriate challenges requiring effortful processing, even though these challenges may temporarily impair performance during training.

Desirable difficulty explains why challenging practice conditions may temporarily reduce performance yet increase durable learning. Practice conditions that make skills temporarily harder to access during training increase how well they're learned, leading to better long-term retention (Bjork & Bjork, 2011).

Conditions that make skills too easy to execute in firearms training may create false confidence and poor retention. Appropriately challenging conditions build robust capabilities that remain accessible under operational stress, though they may appear less satisfying during training. Several training modifications can introduce desirable difficulty into firearms instruction while maintaining safety and learning effectiveness. These modifications should be implemented systematically, carefully maintaining appropriate challenge levels without overwhelming learners or compromising the safety of the learning environment.

Spaced Practice & The Forgetting Benefit

Spaced or distributed practice is one of the most potent elements of desirable difficulty. Spacing is more effective than blocked repetitive practice for long-term retention, even when total practice time is constant. Research consistently demonstrates that spaced practice outperforms massed practice (blocked training) across different skills and populations, with substantial effect (Donovan & Radosevich, 1999). The mechanisms underlying the spacing effect involve both memory consolidation and retrieval practice. Between practice sessions, memories go through consolidation, a process that strengthens and stabilizes what was learned. Additionally, retrieving information after a delay requires more effort than immediate retrieval, and this effortful retrieval strengthens memory traces – improving durability and retention.

Adapting the practice schedule to space sessions has profound effects on learning outcomes that extend far beyond the immediate training period. For example, rather than doing eighty hours of academy firearms training in a two-week block, twenty separate four-hour sessions over five months would be far more beneficial. If in-service training allocates eight hours for a topic, rather than intensive single-day training, spacing one or two-hour sessions over time promotes better potential for learning.

The space between sessions allows temporary forgetting, and when skills are successfully retrieved learning is strengthened. Optimal spacing schedules typically involve expanding intervals—initial sessions might be separated by days, followed by weekly sessions, and then monthly refreshers. This pattern maximizes both acquisition and retention while efficiently using training time.

One of the most counterintuitive aspects of desirable difficulty is that some forgetting during training can enhance learning. When information or skills become temporarily inaccessible, the effort required to retrieve them strengthens the memory trace, making future retrieval more likely and durable (Bjork & Bjork, 2011).

Spacing practice, which allows partial forgetting between sessions, enhances long-term retention compared to massed practice that maintains constant skill accessibility. The temporary performance dips observed at the beginning of spaced sessions represent beneficial challenges that support long-term learning rather than training failures.

Officers may show reduced performance at the beginning of spaced training sessions due to valuable forgetting between sessions. Rather than indicating training shortcomings, this temporary difficulty strengthens the learning process. Instructors should expect these temporary declines as evidence that robust learning is occurring.

Years of firearms training have been delivered to thousands of recipients using the spaced technique. The method is effective, but it requires trust in the process and patience to see the end results. The hardest part is overcoming the emotional tie to immediate gratification for the instructor and the student. It feels hard in the moment, it can sometimes seem as if learning isn't happening or happening quickly enough. Resist the urge to satisfy your current self, the results are long term and it's not about you. It's not about now. It's about your people being as skilled as possible for the long game.

Contextual Interference

Contextual interference is broad term for the mechanism underlying interleaving and variability of practice. The interference occurs when blocked rote repetition is broken by spacing, and variable tasks (Battig, 1979). This interference forces learners to engage in more effortful processing, leading to stronger memory representations and more flexible skill execution capabilities (Lee & Magill, 1983).

When practicing blocked skills, learners can rely on momentum from previous repetitions and may not fully engage the cognitive processes involved in skill selection and execution. Interleaved and varied practice forces repeated engagement of these processes, strengthening both the motor skills themselves and the decision-making capabilities required for appropriate skill application.

For firearms instruction, contextual interference can be introduced using variable practice and the interleaving of skills. These techniques maintain safety while enhancing learning effectiveness.

Variability of Practice

Classic research by Shea and Morgan (1979) demonstrated that while rote blocked practice initially appears more effective, variable practice produces superior retention when tested after delays. When it comes to range training, rather than shooting the same course of fire repeatedly, effective desirable difficulty requires changes in task parameters. This compels officers to adapt their technique to different conditions, building flexible schemas rather than rigid movement patterns. Variable practice initially reduces immediate performance compared to constant practice but produces superior learning outcomes as demonstrated through retention and transfer tests.

For TFS, even on a live fire range, variability can be broad. It might involve practicing at various distances randomly, rather than completing all shots at one distance before moving to another. This forces continuous adaptation and prevents officers from settling into rigid patterns. Use various target types, including full-size silhouettes, reduced-size targets, multiple targets, moving targets, steel, and negative targets. Mix different shooting positions —standing, kneeling, prone, and barricade positions —unpredictably rather than practicing each position separately. This builds adaptability while strengthening individual position skills.

Interleaving Skills

Interleaving involves mixing different skills or problem types within a single practice session, rather than practicing them in separate blocks. Blocked practice creates impressive immediate performance, but as we've established, this performance advantage doesn't translate to learning and often creates false confidence that has significant implications for officers in the real-world. Interleaved practice produces superior retention and transfer capabilities. Practicing different skills in mixed order rather than in blocks creates interference that enhances long-term, durable learning.

Interleaving might involve alternating between TFS and sight use in the same task for firearms training. It could be the requirement to identify and clear malfunctions while working on movement drills rather than practicing each skill separately. Interleaved practice leads to superior retention and transfer of skills, enhancing operational effectiveness. It doesn't have to stop at interleaving firearms skills either. Blending the use of medical equipment and techniques is an easy connection to firearms skills. Tourniquet application, self-care, partner care, drags, carries and extraction techniques are all closely tied skills that provide easy interleaving opportunities. The list is never ending, everything from handcuffing, to driving, knowledge of statutes and department policy can all be easily weaved into firearms training with minimal effort and cost. The overlapping of the skills not only aligns with the nature of the real world (we do not use skills in isolation), but it also adds to the desirable difficulty of the firearms skill development.

Interleaving forces officers to repeatedly engage the cognitive processes involved in skill selection and execution, strengthening decision-making capabilities along with the motor skills themselves. This preparation is particularly valuable for operational situations where officers must rapidly select and execute appropriate techniques based on evolving circumstances.

Implementation Considerations for the Learner

Implementing desirable difficulty requires careful balance between challenge and achievability. Difficulties that are too great can overwhelm learners, creating excessive frustration and potentially impairing motivation. Difficulties that are too small fail to provide the effortful processing that enhances learning.

Individual differences in skill level, experience, and confidence must be considered when implementing desirable difficulty. Those with higher skill levels may benefit from greater challenges than those with limited experience, but all learners benefit from appropriate levels of difficulty. The key is adjusting challenge levels based on individual capabilities while maintaining the basic principle of effortful processing.

Safety considerations are paramount when implementing desirable difficulty in firearms training. All challenges must be implemented within established safety protocols, and difficulties should never compromise basic safety practices. The goal is enhancing learning effectiveness, not creating unnecessary risks.

Monitoring and adjustment are essential for successful implementation of desirable difficulty. Instructors must attentively observe learner responses to training challenges and be prepared to modify challenge levels based on performance and motivation indicators. The optimal level of difficulty will change as learners progress and as individual differences become apparent.

Implementation Considerations for the Training Team

Successfully implementing spacing and interleaving requires careful planning and systematic execution. Training programs must be redesigned to distribute practice over time and mix skills appropriately, while maintaining safety standards and gaining administrative support. The administrative support is quite often one of the biggest logistical hurdles when it comes to implementing any 'new' idea. I appreciate that gaining support from administrators can be harder than the work itself. It may be the biggest challenge you face in this quest.

Schedule redesign represents the most fundamental change required for implementing spacing effects. Rather than concentrating firearms training into intensive blocks, programs should distribute training across multiple sessions with appropriate intervals. This will require coordination with other training requirements and careful management of training resources.

Curriculum restructuring is necessary to implement interleaving effectively. Traditional curricula that teach skills in isolation must be modified to mix skills appropriately while maintaining logical progression and safety standards. This may involve developing new lesson plans, modifying existing exercises, and training instructors in interleaved practice methods.

Instructor preparation is crucial for the successful implementation of these principles. Instructors must understand the theoretical basis for spacing and interleaving and recognize that initial performance may appear worse with these methods. They must be prepared to explain these principles to officers who may question training approaches that seem to make learning more difficult.

Assessment modifications may be necessary to properly evaluate learning under spaced and interleaved conditions. Traditional assessment methods that focus on immediate performance may not capture the long-term benefits of these approaches. Assessment should include delayed testing and evaluation of skill integration capabilities.

All the principles we've covered—spaced practice, interleaving, appropriate feedback, and desirable difficulty tie nicely into the concept of deliberate practice. This approach transforms random training activities into systematic, intentional skill development.

Deliberate Practice: Quality Over Quantity

Anders Ericsson defined the concept of deliberate practice based on his research into expert performance. Deliberate practice provides crucial insights for developing high-level skills in any realm. Unlike routine or casual training, deliberate practice involves specific characteristics that maximize skill development and accelerate the path to expertise.

Defining Deliberate Practice

Ericsson et al. (1993) distinguished deliberate practice from other forms of training through several key characteristics that work together to optimize learning. Deliberate practice involves:

- Specific goals focused on improvement rather than mere repetition
- Ongoing informative feedback that guides performance adjustments
- Repetition and refinement that allow for gradual skill development
- Progressive difficulty increases that maintain appropriate challenge levels
- High levels of concentration and effort that ensure full engagement with the learning process

These principles have been validated across diverse domains, including sports, medicine, and military training (Ericsson, 2008), suggesting broad applicability to firearms instruction.

Deliberate practice differs fundamentally from typical training approaches in several important ways. While routine practice often involves repetition of comfortable skills, deliberate practice focuses on areas of weakness or difficulty. While casual training may be enjoyable and social, deliberate practice requires sustained concentration and effort that can be mentally and physically demanding. Unlike traditional training focused on immediate performance, deliberate practice emphasizes long-term learning and adaptability.

Deliberate practice is a long-term approach to skill advancement. The key principle is 'little and often'—repeatedly engaging in focused practice sessions over months and years rather than attempting intensive but infrequent training blocks.

Applications for Firearms Training

Implementing deliberate practice principles can transform firearms instruction from routine repetition to focused skill development that accelerates learning and builds higher levels of capability. This transformation requires intentional changes to goal setting, feedback provision, practice design, and performance evaluation.

Set Specific Goals: Rather than generic objectives like "improve accuracy," deliberate practice requires specific, measurable goals that focus attention on particular aspects of performance that need improvement. For TFS, appropriate goals might include:

- Achieve 90% hits on an 8-inch target at 15 feet using TFS
- Draw from holster to first accurate TFS shot in under 1.5 seconds
- Maintain TFS accuracy while moving at a normal walking pace

Specific goals serve multiple functions in deliberate practice. They focus on particular aspects of performance, provide clear criteria for success, enable systematic tracking of improvement over time, and maintain motivation by creating achievable yet challenging targets. Goals should be adjusted regularly as skills develop to maintain appropriate challenge levels. This process should be continuous—when a goal is achieved, parameters should be made more demanding, and new goals should be established at properly challenging levels.

These goals also offer flexibility when teaching to a large audience that may broadly range in skill. Someone progressing rapidly can be given a shorter time constraint or a smaller target to hit. Different people can be on the same range, working the same skills, but their challenge or difficulty level is tailored to their ability.

Focus on Weaknesses: Perhaps the most challenging aspect of deliberate practice is the requirement to focus specifically on areas of weakness rather than practicing comfortable skills. Most people naturally gravitate toward practicing skills they already perform well, but this approach limits improvement potential.

Effective deliberate practice requires systematic identification of performance limitations and focused effort to address those areas. For TFS, this might involve extra practice on shooting positions that prove challenging, concentrated work on specific distances where accuracy suffers, or focused attention to technique elements that show inconsistency.

Progressive Difficulty: Deliberate practice involves increasing challenge levels as skills improve, ensuring that practice remains appropriately demanding throughout the learning process. This requires continuous assessment of current capability and adjustment of practice conditions to maintain optimal difficulty. Progressive difficulty in TFS training might involve changes such as:

- Beginning with closer targets and larger acceptable hit zones
- Increase distances and reduce target sizes as skills develop
- Introduce time pressure
- Introduce movement and multiple targets
- Integrate decision-making and tactical skills

The Role of Mental Effort

Deliberate practice requires sustained mental effort that goes beyond simple physical repetition. When practice becomes automatic or routine, learning plateaus occur regardless of the amount of time spent practicing (Ericsson, 2008). This principle explains why experienced officers sometimes struggle to improve their performance despite extensive practice time. Mental effort in firearms training involves conscious attention to:

- Technique details
- Active problem-solving when errors occur
- Continuous monitoring of performance quality
- Systematic technique adjustment based on feedback

This level of engagement can be mentally fatiguing, so deliberate practice sessions are typically shorter than routine practice sessions.

The requirement for mental effort also explains why group training activities may not always constitute deliberate practice. While group training can be valuable for motivation and standardization, the individual attention and customized feedback required for deliberate practice may be challenging to achieve in large group settings. Effective training programs should balance group activities with individualized practice opportunities.

Conclusion

The evidence is clear: effective firearms training requires abandoning comfortable myths in favor of challenging but proven principles

- Spaced practice distributes learning over time to enhance retention
- Interleaved skills training builds adaptability by mixing different techniques within sessions
- Appropriate feedback guides improvement without creating dependency
- Desirable difficulty strengthens learning through productive struggle
- Deliberate practice targets specific weaknesses with focused attention

These principles work together to build officers' robust capabilities in dynamic operational environments.

Instructors should begin implementation by focusing on the highest-impact changes first. Start with spacing practice sessions and introducing interleaving within existing curricula—these modifications require minimal resource investment but yield significant returns. Next, refine feedback delivery to emphasize guidance over evaluation. Finally, intentionally increase training difficulty and incorporate deliberate practice principles. This phased approach allows departments to adapt gradually, building instructor confidence and demonstrating measurable improvements. The training doesn't have to end when the shift is over, empowering our people with the ability to train on their own is a skill multiplier.

Officers can augment formal training through structured, self-directed practice that applies evidence-based principles. When approached systematically, deliberate practice through dry fire exercises offers significant skill development opportunities. Officers should establish clear safety protocols, set specific performance goals, focus on challenging aspects of their performance, and seek feedback through self-assessment or peer evaluation. Gradually increasing complexity mirrors progressive difficulty in formal training, allowing officers to accumulate additional practice hours and maintain proficiency between sessions.

The choice is stark: continue training that feels good but produces fragile skills or embrace methods that challenge learners and create lasting capabilities. Officer safety and public protection depend on making the evidence-based choice. The ultimate goal of evidence-informed firearms instruction is to develop officers who can perform effectively under the full range of conditions they may encounter. By applying these principles, instructors contribute significantly to officer safety, operational effectiveness, and public protection.

CHAPTER 11 - TRAINING TFS

Since the type of training a person initially receives often dictates how well they perform in the future (Schmidt & Lee, 2005; Vickers, 2007) our results suggest that firearms training should change from a process that inadvertently teaches novices to fixate the sights of their own weapon first and the target second, to a type of training that establishes the line of gaze on the target from the outset.....

- Vickers & Lewinski, 2012

TFS and sight use have their rightful place and purpose. Rather than advocating exclusively for one or the other, it's essential to recognize that each method serves a unique function depending on the context. Insisting on only one approach ignores the practical and situational advantages that each approach to aiming can offer. There are plenty of close-quarter contact engagements and contact shots that preclude the ability of an officer to get the gun between their eyes and the person that needs to be shot. Officers do not always need, nor can they always use sights. We're not training for a target shoot on a range; it's a fight for life. Sometimes that is close and ugly.

Figure 23 *Image of a compressed shooting position where a traditional two hand presentation and sight use are not possible*

The ability to present the gun between our eyes and the target is dictated by circumstance. It is undeniable that sometimes, based on position that the officer aims their gun without using their sights - see Figure 23 for an example.

Sometimes sights are used. Sometimes they are not. With that duality of aiming reality accepted, the only real question to be answered is at what distance the transition must occur. Where do sighting systems become the absolute must for aiming versus relying on coupling our vision and motor skills without reference to the sights? The quote from the previous page concludes like this:

.... followed by alignment of the sights of the weapon to the line of gaze. This change in gaze control would lead to a longer quiet eye duration on the target prior to pulling the trigger and should contribute to better decision-making and performance.

- Vickers & Lewinski, 2012

I break that quote from Vickers and Lewinski into two parts as a representation for how I recommend teaching people to aim the handgun. When teaching handgun aiming, I recommend starting by focusing vision entirely on the target. This approach helps build trust in one's ability to aim while also developing competence in gun manipulation. Then, with a foundation established, complexity can be layered:

- Increased speed and recoil management
- Movement before and while drawing the gun
- Working from various ready positions
- Breaking and rebuilding grip with the use of reloads and malfunction clearance skill builders

All those tasks are completed with 100% focus on the target, all within 15 feet. Then, sights and distance come into play.

Vision and attention are expected to remain on the target. The addition of sights is a progression from the foundation. The sights are attended to after being brought into the shooter's visual field; however, the shooter should remain target-focused whilst using their sighting system; more on that later.

Throughout training, both sighted and unsighted aiming methods should be regularly revisited and merged through tasks that allow shooters to choose between the approaches based on the distance, difficulty of the target, and their own skill level. This approach empowers shooters to make informed decisions about the most suitable aiming technique for each situation, simultaneously building their adaptability and decision-making skills.

That's a high-level overview of the process. The following section will offer some suggestions for how to break it down and for the rationale behind some of the drills used to build skills, also including the why behind the suggestion. These are not a rigid set of TFS commandments. Coaching is as much of an art as it is a science. I respect that some readers will want to adapt the sequence or even disregard some of the steps that do not work for them and their training goals. This is what I have found to be successful for tangible results in performance-based assessment, robust transferable skills, as well as for student buy-in and trust in the process. They also have fun on the learning journey too, which is an important objective for me!

Foundational or Advanced Skill?

Target-focused shooting is absolutely a foundational skill. People who talk about needing thousands of repetitions of regular sight use before progressing to target-focused shooting have never tried it. The speed at which this can be learned by a novice is one of the reasons why Fairbairn and Applegate used this as the core training for members of the units that would become the Special Air Service (SAS) and the Central Intelligence Agency (CIA). There are many good reasons to start at close range (10-12 feet) with absolute TFS and no reference to the sighting system. These are the two most important reasons:

1. It's how we are going to ask people to operate in the real world

The justification for employing deadly force will originate from external stimuli. It is highly likely to be visual, but not exclusively. Teaching people from the very beginning to direct their vision and attention outward is crucial. TFS is a way to set that expectation as a functional foundation.

We are training people to be prepared to work while experiencing fear, for themselves and/or for others. Fear drives attention to the threat, and it drives it there quickly. This is a deep-rooted human attribute predicated upon survival. This subconscious hijacking of vision and attention can be reliably and repeatedly proven in a lab with a simple picture of something scary (De Oca &

Black, 2013; Trujillo et al., 2021). If we know a reflexive attention shift is likely to happen, this is how we should be developing training and skills.

Task-relevant information is always going to be the key to success. Knowing where to look and when to look there is the hallmark of a high performer. For law enforcement officers, that visual information is most likely to come from the subject. That is where we should be training vision and attention, right from the first minutes of a training program.

2. It's simpler

If you've been doing anything for a while, you develop comfort with it. You likely forget how taxing it was when you first learned to shoot. For a novice, just getting the gun out of the holster and bringing it up between their eyes and the target is a big and possibly scary task. Add to that the likely overwhelming nature of trying to remember all the safety rules they were subjected to and the laundry list of 'fundamentals' that they have been told are crucial to success. It is a lot to try to hold in working memory. The skills and knowledge that you draw on effortlessly as an experienced practitioner and instructor are not something available to a new shooter. Every new action for them is an effortful application of attention and recall from short term memory. Both of those resources have a very finite limit.

For those of you who have taught new shooters, have you ever watched them completely forget the last thing you taught them when introduced to the next new thing? Ever observed a shooter who has never moved their feet and drawn their gun at the same time, fail when asked to follow that simple request? Normally, we see them separate the tasks. They often either stand still, draw, then move – or move, then draw. For the casual observer, it can be both funny and frustrating, depending on our mood. They are not usually trying to fail or frustrate you; this is just what it looks like when someone is trying to juggle something new for the first time. This comes back to attentional capacity and the concept of switch tasking covered earlier in chapter 7. Keeping the first steps into handgun shooting simpler is a way to respect the attentional limits of a daunting task.

The real long-term benefit here is the honing of attention from the start. Using this process, the target is always going to get visual attention first. Vision will always be intrinsically linked to the decisions people make operationally. TFS, as the first steps in the learning process, builds that robust transferable habit, skill, and expectation from the start.

TFS has been used as the day one aiming process for thousands of law enforcement officers. It has been used as a handgun introduction for responsible citizens who have never shot a gun before – they are incredibly successful at it. People with no handgun experience are the easiest to teach–

they have no misconceptions to break down. They haven't been told never and always. Skill progression and confidence develop more quickly without initially relying on sighting systems to aim. When target difficulty is introduced, the transition feels more natural. As the aiming tasks become more challenging (for example, by increasing distance or reducing target size), that is the appropriate time to introduce additional layers to the aiming process.

The rapidity of progression and confidence outstrips a sighted start process. When sights and distance are added, it flows more as a natural progression. As the aiming tasks get more difficult by adding distance or reducing target size, it is time to add another layer to the aiming process.

People are exponentially more likely to miss because of the unnecessary movement they introduce during the trigger press when using sights than if they had no sights at all. Rather than moving just the trigger, shooters move the entire gun. I have watched people miss their intended target area by two feet while using sights from just a few yards away. I have never seen anyone be that far from their intended target area using an unsighted TFS approach. It sounds oxymoronic, but sights can make people less accurate if they do not know how to move a trigger first. The unnecessary movement of the whole gun when trying to manipulate just the trigger is far more influential to handgun accuracy than the alignment of sights. Teach people to aim with vision on the target, move the trigger without moving the gun, and everything else that follows will be easier.

TFS From the Holster?

….. in my experience, the demonstrations of point shooting by its advocates are generally neither from the holster nor against a moving suspect, both of which are the rule when drawing from a startle response against a real attacker.

- Mroz, 2000

I have always been a proponent of this technique being relevant for what may ineloquently be referred to as an 'Oh, shit!' moment. When an officer is startled and thrust into an impromptu close-quarter fight for life, TFS is a normal and often reflexive response (Kantor et al., 2024). In this high-consequence, time and distance compressed context, falling back to Fairbairn's first principle is the answer to the question of what to practice – extreme speed in drawing and firing (Fairbairn et al., 1942). In proximity, even untrained opponents present a significant threat in their speed and their accuracy (Kantor et al., 2022; Lewinski et al., 2015).

Target-focused shooting should absolutely be worked from the holster and every other conceivable ready position. TFS can be applied to moving targets; it can be used by a shooter who is on the move, or both. The context of the environment drives the applicability of TFS. It is a process of aiming the gun when speed is necessary, and the accuracy demands of the task are within acceptable limits. This is often referred to as a balance of speed and accuracy.

Using the TFS model to teach the draw from the holster is a powerful place to start. As you are probably (hopefully) noticing by now, vision and attention are core concepts for maximizing information-gathering potential. The more skilled officers become at assessing their environment, the better they will become at detecting and responding to problems they encounter. Training them from the outset to look at what they intend to point a gun at and bring that gun to their line of sight without looking down at the gun is optimal (Vickers & Lewinski, 2012).

Learning to access the gun from the holster can begin on a range. Ideally, it could happen in a more contextually rich environment (see Get off the range). Learning to draw does not have to be done standing still in a neat line with an unnatural stimulus. With an unloaded gun, it can be done anywhere there is an appropriate direction to point the firearm. If you have substitute equipment, draw training can be even more reality-based. When I say substitute equipment, I mean an inert replica of some form. Whether that is a molded block of plastic that is handgun-shaped, or something that is a little higher tech, like the Mantis TitanX, is down to preference or availability. The inert options expand the opportunity for training diversity.

Close Your Eyes, Shoot the Gun

Shooting with eyes closed can seem like an odd place to start - but there is method to the madness! Whether the shooter is brand new to handgun use or they are just new to the concept of TFS, this is a proven starting point. It must be performed close to the target for the first iterations - about six feet away to avoid muzzle blast shredding the paper, but no further. The demonstration and the explanation are key to this being an opportunity for learning and discovery. If this is pitched poorly or incorrectly, it has the potential to be a detrimental experience. If it is done the right way, with the students learning in mind, this can be a significant self-discovery moment. I have included my suggested outline for the drill at the end of this section. Shooting with eyes closed needs an introduction; it needs the trainer to solidly establish why it is occurring. These are the two most important reasons I recommend starting with this:

1. *It focuses on physical technique*

Typically, when we shoot at the range, the external feedback from the target is influential in our self-assessment. If the holes in the paper are where we want them to be, then we consider that to be success. We may be succeeding despite fundamental flaws in how we support and present the handgun. An extreme example of sights allowing for suboptimal control of the gun would be an upside-down handgun shooting party trick (see Figure 24). That type of showmanship will confirm a gun will shoot at any angle. It will demonstrate that unconventional control of the gun can be used for a single round fired in an infinite amount of time. That doesn't mean the technique is viable, or readily repeatable at any level of efficiency. It would be useless to teach as an operational skill.

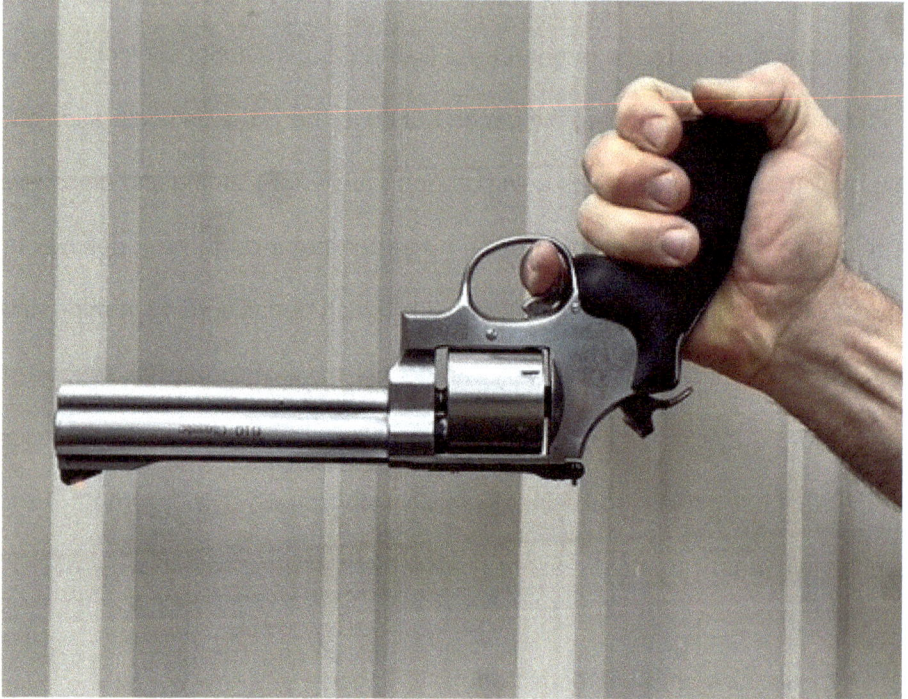

Figure 24 *Image of a handgun being shot upside down*

Firing a gun upside down would create, at best, a fragile illusion of success. The illusion would be easily dismissed when the technique was put to the test. So, keep in mind that just because a target is hit, it doesn't mean the process used is useful or worthy.

Vision is a dominant sense when using a sighting system to aim, and it eats up our attentional resources. When vision is removed from the process, by closing our eyes, it allows us to concentrate on other sensory input. Remember attentional filtering from a few chapters ago? We can harness attentional filtering to enhance our diagnostic process.

If the shooter has their eyes closed, they are more easily able to focus on feel without distraction. Does the recoil of the gun get to change their grip or move their body around? If people are leaning backward as they shoot, their toes will start to lift off the floor when the handgun fires. A 9mm pistol can make an adult's toes lift from the ground and disrupt their entire sense of balance and stability. This is not because of the awesome power of that caliber, but more because they weren't setting themselves up for success with their posture. Attentional filtering means with their eyes open they ordinarily did not notice the issue of weight distribution. They can routinely and unknowingly practice with a detrimental technique, but because the sights on the handgun allow them to compensate whilst simultaneously soaking up their attention, they have never noticed. Shooting with eyes closed allows people to concentrate on what's happening with their body and feel what happens when the gun is fired. That internal attentional focus leads to awareness and the opportunity to improve technique.

Leveraging a narrow internal focus of attention at the right time is extremely useful for skill development. Internal attentional focus should be used intentionally in training and development for reasons just like this. Internal attention isn't commensurate with great skill performance in the operational realm. Internal attention is extremely useful for training essential elements. It is best used as a transitional state of mind, intended to be temporary, not prolonged. Once the necessary adjustments have been identified and made, attention needs to be prioritized back to external.

The use of the directed internal focus while shooting with closed eyes serves as a subtle separation, too. It helps to keep the principle of maximal external focus on the pedestal it deserves. Shooters will spend very little time working on skills with their eyes closed. Comparatively, they should also spend very little time thinking internally when shooting.

Prior to completing the live fire drill, the 'why' should be discussed. The purpose of shooting the gun without looking is to focus on self-assessing stance and grip without visual distraction. The shooter should focus on feedback from the gun. Does recoil affect weight distribution through the feet and/or hand position on the gun? If so, these must be adjusted.

2. *It builds trust in the technique*

I quite often use the eyes-closed introduction in two stages. It keeps things easy to follow, and it helps to allow a little discovery for the learner. The eyes closed technique is a great approach for self-diagnosis, and I use this explanation to clarify its purpose before people undertake the task. Once they have completed that task and there are some holes in the target, it opens the door for another perspective.

All shooters will have produced a consistent shot group of some kind. Even with their eyes closed and after the gun moved (recoiled) several times, there will be a consistency with shot placement once they have established how to use their body optimally. The consistency in their shot placement serves as the key to establishing trust in the process. As this is potentially a big 'ah ha' moment for the shooters, I like to try and understand their thought process. I use questions to make the connection.

I like to teach through questions whenever possible. Answering a question requires people to think about what they have done or what they are about to do; it also personalizes the experience and creates buy-in to something they may not have ever done before. In addition, asking questions helps to cut through the illusion of learning (Carey, 2015). If I just issue a list of endless instructions, people end up mindlessly and blindly doing what they've been told. I will never really be sure if they understand what they're doing, how, or why they are doing it. So, for that reason, my question to the students at that point is, "How did you create consistent shot placement without a visual reference, even after the gun moved?" Don't be one of those instructors who ask and answer all their own questions – wait for them to think and respond! The answers should generally have the same underlying principle, even though they don't have to use specific words to explain it. They are all likely to be circling around the idea that they used their body to aim and control the position of the handgun.

With that epiphany moment captured, ask them if they believe they could still be consistent if they took a step or two back and were allowed to keep their eyes open?

The Eyes Closed Drill

Draw and present (eyes open). Verify the gun is aimed at the intended area of the target. Close eyes, and fire six rounds, keeping eyes closed throughout. When the six rounds have been fired, the shooter should open their eyes. Holster the pistol and consider what they felt. Although there will be holes in the target, those aren't the primary source of feedback at this point. How the gun movement influenced their control of the gun is the priority. The shooter should make any necessary changes, then repeat the drill with another six rounds to confirm those changes.

If additional repetitions are required, this is where the art of coaching comes into play. There is no magic number that can be written for how many is enough. If you're teaching multiple people at once, they will be spread across a range of skill levels. Tailor your teaching to their abilities. Be mindful of round counts and magazine capacity. The gun running out of ammunition in the middle of this drill may disrupt the intention behind it. The shooter breaking their flow and concentration during this very focused initial self-assessment is less than ideal.

Once everyone is finished, discuss the findings with the shooters and what they discovered and adjusted. This follow-up discussion requires the shooters to explain what they felt and what they changed. This helps them to understand their decisions and allows you to assess their understanding.

Permission to Miss? Seriously?

I will preface this section with a reminder that safe and responsible gun handling is an uncompromising need. It is not negotiable.

When training people to shoot, there is often a stigma associated with missing. Missing is a relative term, and I do not intend to minimize or excuse safety concerns. I make no excuse for the person shooting the floor or errantly into the sky. In this context of missing, I am referring to the soul-crushing self-imposed shame when a shooter leaves an arbitrarily designated score zone on the target. When their round 'misses' the circle, their world crumbles, their confidence and performance spiral, and growth is stifled. The greatest shooters on the planet miss. Anyone who tells you they have never missed is either a liar or has never shot a gun. As you may recall from the chapter on learning, for us to grow, we need to find our limits, train to them, and sometimes push beyond them.

When starting out with TFS, you should keep the shooters close to the target to build confidence. 9–12 feet is the sweet spot for the first drills. People who have exclusively trained in sight use need to be given permission to miss or allow their groups to 'open up'. They probably won't even need to use the permission you gave them to miss. It is highly unlikely they will miss the target and just shoot the berm or backstop. Thousands of students have completed these introductory drills on a live fire range, and I've never seen a shot leave the paper, even though permission was given to do so. With that permission comes the freedom to learn through discovery. A crucial part of the leap of faith in breaking from dogma is the confidence that there will be no reprimand for missing a dot, a circle, or a bullet hole as they begin their learning journey.

I've learned through extensive personal research and experience that you have to say this out loud. As people try this out for the first time, you must tell them it is ok if they miss. Whether you are training a novice, an experienced tactical whizz, or other instructors, you cannot imply it or assume. It must be said specifically and understood by the shooter. It takes no more than about 20 seconds to say it. The impact on people's engagement and their subsequent success is huge. If you don't say it, people will still apply their point-scoring mentality. They will try to use all the available time to create the smallest group possible. For the sake of your shooter's success on the line and in the field, just say it and mean it.

If you don't say it, they will try to stare at the back of the gun; they will try to use the edge of the slide to aim. They will do all this just a few feet from the target because they have been so conditioned that they must produce a single hole style shot group. The irony is, those who try to stare at the gun to aim are slower and less accurate than those who just take a leap of faith. When they join me on the journey of exploration that is TFS, they see better, faster results.

The First Shots

The first live fire shots of TFS are an important confidence builder. The drills I include here are recommended approaches to start this journey when working on a live fire range. Also included are considerations for you, as the coach, taking people through the steps. All we're doing is changing what they look at and how they aim. Your skills as a coach will carry over to this aiming technique; you don't need new ones. You will likely see a few common missteps captured in the coaching tips that follow the drill outline. These are offered to help you be primed to recognize issues and offer guidance to your shooters.

The Single Shot Drill

This drill starts with a draw from the holster. The target should be blank/plain. It should have no score zones or areas marked. Shooters should be somewhere between 9 and 12 feet from the target. Shooters will focus their vision on a specific area at the center of the target. Both eyes remain open. When the drill begins, they will draw and press the gun toward the spot they are focusing on. Immediately upon completing the press out to full extension, they will fire one round. There should be no delay once the pistol is presented. That first bullet hole is now their target. Wherever else the subsequent shots go, they should remain focused on that first centrally located visual reference point: the first bullet hole.

When they are ready, the gun should be returned to the holster, and the drill repeated. As the coach, it is your call how many reps they shoot, but usually somewhere between ten and twenty rounds provides the opportunity to assess people's grasp of the idea.

The Multiple Shots Drill

Building from the single-shot drill, the next progression is multiple shots. There should be no push for speed between shots yet. The stimulus for each subsequent shot will be the gun returning to where it was. Much like the eyes closed drill, after the gun recoils and then settles back where it was prior to the shot breaking, the trigger should be pressed again. Repeated shots can allow for micro adjustments from the shooter in how they grip and aim. Using bullet holes in this early stage of learning can provide immediate feedback on their control of the handgun.

The shooters should fire more than one round each time they draw, but less than five. Let them work on that in their own time for multiple repetitions. Your judgment and the art of coaching come into play again for how long you do this before progressing. A minimum of thirty rounds is recommended, spread through numerous iterations of fire and with varied round counts. Please don't give them "draw and fire two" repeatedly. The most prolific training scar created on ranges is the perpetuation of two rounds. If you've never noticed it, start looking and listening for it. Two rounds is a firearms instructor's favorite number. Help me break the futile fascination with pairs; let the shooters choose and vary their round count.

The Varied Start Positions Drill

The next progression is to vary the start position. The draw from the holster is probably the most common presentation for law enforcement. Ready positions are typically practiced less. Adding high/low ready start positions is an important part of the skill-building process. Whatever your agency or department designates as a high and/or low ready is what you should use. TFS will work from wherever the gun comes from. You don't need to adjust your preparatory tactics or techniques.

Continue with the multiple shots approach. Allow the shooters to work in their own time, varying how many rounds they fire in each iteration. The only difference between this and the previous drill is the start position. Their ability to hold consistent shot groups should not be affected. At least twice as many rounds should be spent on this as you allocated to the prior multiple shots drill. Once again, your skills as a coach will determine when they're ready to progress.

First Shots Coaching Tips

Keep the targets as clean as possible. Tape holes regularly or replace targets completely, if you prefer. Barring a safety concern, these drills are best run without coaching while they are shooting. Don't interrupt the shooter during the drill if you notice a shot or two that varies from the rest of their work. Give them the time to feel their way through the process and make their own micro adjustments. Coaching should come between iterations. The exception to that is if everything they are shooting is inconsistent and scattered; that is a flaw that needs your attention. The most common causes are these:

- Vision and Attention are not focused on a consistent spot on the target – this results in a larger, more scattered grouping

- They are the last ones to shoot. They are likely trying to use the gun to aim, which defeats the purpose

- They do not let the gun stop moving before they fire it—this usually presents as high hits from the holster or the low ready. It presents as low hits from the high ready

- Rushing to come off target and holster/returning to low ready as they fire. Sometimes their self-induced need for speed means they do everything fast. This miss commonly manifests as low/scattered hits

Always leave them a bullet hole to focus on for these first iterations. It helps them get used to being target-focused and provides something to focus their vision and attention on. That focus of vision and attention should be purposefully intense. Eventually, using a bullet as a target will be phased out. Remember, the end goal is training for life. Operationally, there will not be holes in paper targets to stare at. Use the visual aid of a bullet hole as a day one training aid, then move on.

TFS and Recoil Management

Teaching for speed first and then providing an accuracy constraint, only when a skilled pattern has emerged, should provide the greatest benefit in terms of acquiring more advanced movement patterns as well as promoting consistency and accuracy.

- Molina et al., 2019

The prior dills should have served a purpose for both coach and shooter. Deliberate single shots and untimed multiple shots should have the shooter feeling confident in their ability to aim the gun without the use of a sighting aid. The drills should also have provided coaches with the opportunity to assess performance and provide guidance for any improvement opportunities.

Sustained recoil management harnessed in the right context will allow the gun to be a source of feedback for the shooter. The next drill discussed is called the accelerator, and it offers the opportunity attain feedback while building trust and confidence in how efficient and accurate TFS aiming can be. The drill uses recoil to assess the shooter's fundamentals. It will highlight if a pistol caliber round has the power to shift grip or move the shooter's whole body around. If that is happening, there is still some fundamental aspect(s) of grip, stance and posture that need adjustment.

Everyone will have a different speed limit at which they can accurately shoot their pistol. Each person's target will 'tell them' how efficiently they can aim and manage recoil with their current skills.

The Accelerator Drill (speed limit finder)

This drill can start from a ready position or from the holster. I would encourage multiple repetitions with varied start positions. The target should be blank/plain. It should have no score zones or areas marked. Shooters should be somewhere between 9 and 12 feet from the target. Shooters will focus their vision on a specific area at the center of the target (a small mark from a sharpie or other tiny visual aid to help focus is an option). Both eyes remain open. When the drill begins, they will draw and press the gun toward the spot they are focusing on. Immediately upon completing the press out to full extension, they will fire one round. There should be no delay once the pistol is presented. That first bullet hole is now their target. Wherever else the subsequent shots go, they should remain focused on that first centrally located visual reference point.

The second shot should not be rushed, when the gun returns to where it was, the shooter should fire a round. The third shot should be taken with less of a delay than the second. The delay between shot three and four should be less than it was between shot two and three. This decrease in time between shots should continue for an entire magazine. The final shots should have much less time between them than the first ones did. It should sound like a very deliberate and gradual increase in speed.

The only reason the speed should not be incrementally increased is if the target tells the shooter to slow down. This feedback will come in the form of shot placement and group size. I restrict the acceptable group size to about the size of a football – English or American footballs are the shooter's choice. If the shooter's group grows beyond that size, they must stop, reset, and start again from the beginning, incrementally building pace again. If the group stays within that area, they just keep accelerating.

This drill is a powerful self-discovery opportunity. It is not uncommon for people to be astounded that the accelerator drill allows them to shoot faster and more accurately than ever before. I would encourage at least two repetitions, more if you have the time and resources.

The accelerator drill will show people what their speed limit is with a gradual buildup. It is a very individualized discovery. Once that has been established, it is time to pressure test their discovery.

The Bill Drill (speed limit pressure tester)

The bill drill requires the shooter to present the handgun and fire six rounds at <u>their</u> speed limit. There is no buildup for this drill; they fire all six rounds at the pace they discovered at the end of the accelerator.

This can begin with a draw from the holster or from a ready position of their choice – keep it varied. The drill should initially be completed at the same distance used for the accelerator. The acceptable level of accuracy is the football-sized group used for the accelerator. The target can be new or used, though if used, any prior hits outside of the football-sized group should be taped up/repaired.

Repeat this drill as required.

Variations to the bill drill

The basic drill can be challenging enough on its own. However, a few ways exist to vary it and increase its complexity to keep your shooters challenged and avoid the training scar of doing the same thing repeatedly:

- Increase the distance
- Use a target repeatedly so it becomes distractingly full of holes
- Put clothing over the target, a T-shirt for example and assess aiming ability without the reference of holes in paper
- Use a target with a score zone (based on performance)
- Complete it in low, altered, or failing light
- Add inert training rounds to the magazines to induce malfunctions, compelling attentional shift, and grip breakdown/reestablishment
- Require movement before, during, or after the shots are taken

TFS and Movement

Plenty of compelling reasons necessitate movement in real life. There are two areas to focus on when it comes to movement and shooting. The first is moving, then shooting, which is like playing checkers. The second is moving and shooting simultaneously, which can feel a little more like three-dimensional chess. With no known study about which type of movement is the most prolific in law enforcement encounters, it is tough to put a ratio on their occurrence. It's hard to say that moving and then shooting is more common than shooting on the move, as both circumstances are prominent.

Even to a casual observer of the unfortunate number of videos available of officer-involved shootings, it does seem highly likely that some movement is going to be involved before, during, or after the event. The suggestions I offer for movement techniques here can be applied to the use of sighted fire just as they can for TFS and moving. The best practices for moving are equally applicable for aiming, regardless of type. These techniques are designed to maximize handgun stability. If you need to refine the aiming process through sight use, you will still reap huge reward by starting with stabilizing your shooting platform.

If I get to choose whether to shoot on the move or whilst stationary, I will choose stationary every day of the week, and twice on Sundays. No one shoots faster and more accurately when they are moving. Shooting on the move can be done, and it can be done very well. Nevertheless, it is more difficult than standing still. With that said, the question often arises about how to keep the gun steadily pointed at the target without a sighting system to assure it. It's a valid question, but you've been training for this your whole life, you just didn't know it.

The ability to shoot on the move is taught in several ways. I've heard everything from walk like Groucho Marks to walk like a duck. Most young people have no idea who Marks is, and ducks waddle, which is the opposite of the body movement I would consider optimal. Both of those seem like poor examples to me. I've heard better advice, too, but my preferred approach is to try to give people a broader perspective on why they need to adapt their way of walking. The goal is to keep the upper body and, by extension, the gun, as stable as possible. That's why we need to think about how we walk differently when shooting. When individuals understand the goal and reasoning behind required adjustments, they are better equipped to take responsibility for implementing changes in a personally effective manner, thereby enhancing their potential for success. Our regular walk has a little bounce to it, which can make aiming harder, whether with sights or without.

The key to effective stabilization lies in utilizing the lower body, beginning at the hips, to provide a stable foundation for the upper body. Breaking that down further, the length of stride matters; shorter step length reduces the change in elevation. The distance between our feet matters; the closer they are in placement when they touch the ground, the less side-to-side movement we see. Flexion in the ankles, knees, and hips is a factor that changes the way we impact the ground and that matters. Our foot strike should be closer to a stealthy walk across a creaky floorboard versus the angry stomp of a petulant child. This softer strike reduces the potential for a jolt through our body each time we place a foot. Earlier I mentioned that you've already been training for this; here's how.

For those of you with kids at home, imagine this scene. It's early morning, you and your significant other are awake before you would like to be. You're both tired and in need of a caffeine boost. You are the hero of this story. You bravely crossed a Lego-littered floor and went to the kitchen. Once there, you made coffee so powerfully strong the spoon you used to stir it could almost stand up on its own. You filled each cup to the brim for maximum caffeine deployment. Then, the most demanding part of your mission begins. You must carry the steaming hot beverages back to your safe haven. As you negotiate the perilous journey you are doing all the things you need for successful shooting on the move. You are using every part of your body from the hips down to stabilize everything from the hips up. You may also be using a little arm suspension, too.

For those readers who are younger or with a different lifestyle, just picture yourself walking across a crowded bar. In your hands is a tray with a dozen shots of Fireball, or perhaps, if you're classy, you're carrying a tray of champagne glasses. Maybe none of these are you. Maybe you have another life skill to reference, carrying things you don't want to spill. Whatever you've been carrying, the way you adapt your movement for stability is a baseline for how to move and shoot.

Figure 25 *Image of a person carrying a tray of drinks across a Lego covered floor - highlighting an extreme example of existing learned skills to maintain stability during movement*

Those principles of stability will apply to successfully shooting on the move, whether using a sighting system or TFS to aim. I encourage starting with rearward movement when teaching TFS as the aiming process. Rearward is the least optimal directional choice, if you have one. Moving rearward means you can't see where you're going, we move more slowly backward, and eventually, you will probably fall over. Sometimes, the world doesn't work the way we want it to, and we must function within the constraints we face. Sometimes, the only option will be to move backward, down a narrow hallway, an alleyway, or retreating to cover behind a cruiser. Context will drive the need and direction for movement. Training should include preparation for all directions.

Starting with rearward movement is a carrot-and-stick experience for the learner. The stick is that they are going backwards, which is always going to feel like the harder way to learn. The carrot is that they are starting close. Close starts provide the opportunity for a confidence-building step into shooting and moving TFS style.

I would suggest they start about an arm's length from the target. TFS feels natural here. When the stimulus or cue is presented, the movement rearward and the draw should occur simultaneously. By the time the gun is up and presented, they will be far enough away that live fire muzzle blast won't cause a target to shred. Keep the first reps short, just two or three steps before resetting. When success is apparent, add a step for each rep. See how far people can move before the technique starts to falter. It is often surprising that people move and shoot consistently once they get 'set' on the target. If their body mechanics are solid, you should see people easily holding a consistent group out to fifteen feet or more.

Wherever the limit is set for that rearward movement, it can now become the starting point for the introduction of the forward movement. Keep the shooters close to build the skill and confidence for the introduction—no more than a car length for the first repetitions. The same move-and-draw-simultaneously approach should be applied here. They should stop moving forward about six feet from the target. Your carrot and stick are now reversed. The forward movement will be easier and more natural; the shooting will be more challenging as they start further away. But they have already shown they can successfully hit the target at this distance while walking backward. The achievability of this distance was predetermined with rearward movement.

The final stage of closed skill style movement would be oblique rearward movement. This is much like the rearward movement as far as the skills used to stabilize the body. This won't feel any different, but it will look different. The visual difference becomes apparent when this drill is done on a paper target. If a paper target remains stationary as the shooter moves backward at an angle, it starts to appear as if the paper is narrowing. This exposes a disconnect from practical, real-life context. Human opponents are far more likely to orientate their body toward you. If you start to move at an angle, they are likely to mirror that movement to maintain their attack, to pursue you, or both. In that respect the narrowing target does not correlate to the likely outcomes of reality. The win from a training perspective is the target angle now presents a novel area of aim. It creates the experience of seeing a new and apparently shape-changing target while on the move without any special equipment.

That serves as a blueprint for a live fire introduction to the concept of how to move and shoot while aiming with TFS. If you recall, my first steps into the realm of TFS were actual steps. I first consciously did it while on the move with non-lethal marking rounds. There's no reason that this must start on a live fire range. Live fire must be done at some point; it doesn't have to be first, though. There are numerous ways to make this introduction to TFS on the move more interesting by incorporating realistic environments, along with stimuli and adversaries that help build mental models of what to look for, while integrating decision-making experience into the process.

TFS and Multiple Targets

The basic technique remains the same except that both eyes are kept open and focused fully on the target.

-   Greenwood, 1966

Shooting at multiple targets is another area of pressure testing the technique. Unless you've seen it or tried it, transitioning from target to target can seem like a sighting necessity – it isn't. There's a rudimentary test we can run to get an idea of the existing skill transfer we harness with TFS and engaging multiple targets. It starts by choosing something to point at, and then a second thing to transition to. Right now, I am typing this while sitting at an airport departure gate. There is a large TV mounted by the door to the plane showing the flight details. On the adjacent wall, there is a large symbol of the operating airline's logo. Those are my two 'targets' for the test.

Staring at the TV, I simply point my dominant hand, index finger extended toward it. Then, I leave my hand where it's pointed and move my eyes and head so I am staring at the logo. Then, when my eyes arrive, I bring my finger across and point at my new visual focus. Go ahead, try it out. Try it a few times; try it on various objects in your surroundings. You are now officially trained in target transitions.

Our ability to point has been honed over a lifetime. You learned to reach out and point before you learned to speak or even crawl (Arnet & Jensen, 2019). If you played along with the multi-target pointing test just now, I'll bet you were confident in knowing you were pointing toward what you were looking at. The look first, then point technique is stable and reliable. Whether aiming is done with sights or TFS there is a common error that occurs. People try to move their gun, head and eyes all at the same time. This approach leads to shots arriving early or late. By early or late I mean the shot is taken prior to arriving at the intended point of aim, or after unintentionally passing it.

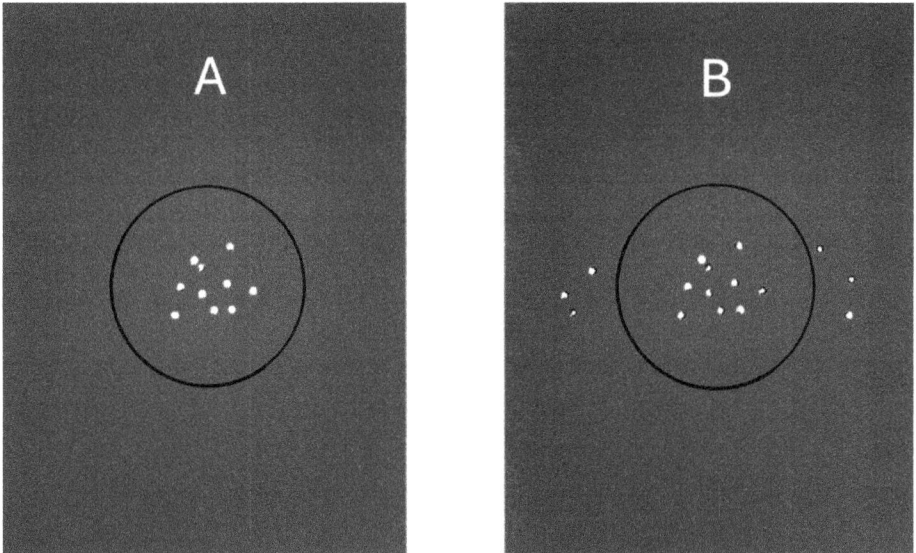

Figure 26 Image of two targets, labelled A & B, each with an 8-inch circular score zone marked. Target B shows the outcome when a shooter transitions and shoots too early (before getting on target) or passing the intended target and shooting beyond the intended target

Figure 26 shows two targets, A & B. The shooter started on target A and transitioned to target B. They were transitioning from left to right. The shots that arrive 'early' are the ones to the left side of target B. Those shots were taken before the shooter had completed their aiming movement. The shots that are to the right of target B were made by the shooter traveling past their intended target.

The key to success with learning target transitions is to look first, then bring your hands/gun along afterward. This can be done almost simultaneously, but we need to settle our vision on what we want to aim at. I advise separating the two movements in the very early stages of practicing this technique. Move the head/eyes, then move the gun. When using sights, the confirmation of muzzle position can be verified by sight use, even though that should, in theory, eliminate the early or late shots, it does not. The same error is committed frequently, regardless of how the gun is being aimed (sights or TFS). The error is the gun doesn't stop. People are trying to time the shot as they go past the target. They either press the trigger too early or too late. Just like the mantra for trusting TFS on those first few shots from the holster, the advice to solve this problem is the same - when the gun stops moving, press the trigger.

When you're moving the gun from one static target to another static target, the gun needs to stop moving before you take the shot. This simple piece of guidance is going to fix most errors you see with the early and late shooters (with or without sights). When they miss early or late it is because they are pressing the trigger when the gun is on the move and trying to guestimate to capture the moment when it passes across the target. It's very unreliable and inaccurate. The gun coming to a halt is key.

New TFS practitioners are going to see quick success following this sequence. By looking where they want to shoot, bringing the gun to match their visual point of focus, letting the gun stop moving, and then pressing the trigger. The transition from one static target to another is simple. As the shooter builds skill and confidence, those steps blend into one sequence. That is the goal. The skilled practitioner will make the transition appear like a singular fluid motion. It is not going to look like the gun is stopping, then shooting. It is going to look like it is happening instantaneously.

TFS and Dry Fire

The practice I advise, is to point suddenly, even with your finger, at objects, when you are alone, and then, shutting one eye, to look along it, before you alter its situation, to ascertain if your aim has been correct or not: by practising this for some time you will acquire much skill before you resort to the same practice with a pistol.

- Lt Col Baron De Berenger, 1835

Dry fire practice can be a tremendous skill-building tool when used effectively. Building confidence and competence in remaining target-focused and pointing the gun does not have to be done exclusively at a range or during structured department-mandated training. As my old friend De Berenger suggests, at a rudimentary level, practicing your ability to point can be done anywhere without needing equipment.

De Berenger would have probably enjoyed the tech options that have become available since he wrote his book. A molded handgun replica could enhance his dry-fire pointing drill with 100% safety. This addition allows practitioners to feel a true replica of their gun's shape and grip angle in their hands as they practice pointing it. Confirmation of aiming can be made with the sighting system on the molded gun, as desired. A small laser could be mounted to the accessory rail beneath the slide if visual confirmation or tracking of the muzzle benefits the shooter's development (see Figure 27).

Figure 27 An inert molded plastic replica of a handgun with a laser attached. Allowing the user to reference where the muzzle is directed during dry fire practice

Dry fire with an operational firearm would be another option. The risk factor with this approach to dry fire is the reliability of the human operator. Have they ensured that the live gun is unloaded? The injuries and deaths during 'dry fire' with live guns suggest that the obvious isn't that obvious. There is a false sense of overconfidence apparent in many gun users; law enforcement is no exception. Complacency may be one of the contributing factors to the perpetual unintended discharges that plague law enforcement (O'Neill et al., 2018). Casual and casualty aren't far apart in the dictionary or the profession. Dry fire is a safe way to train if there is a competent, mindful professional behind the trigger who ensures the gun is unloaded and stays that way.

Using a dry fire magazine enhances this process tremendously (see Figure 28). The combination of the live firearm and the training magazine allows the shooter to work with their real gun and manipulate the trigger repeatedly without the need to work the slide manually. If desired, this can also be run with a laser to track and confirm muzzle position. The gun sighting system can also be used to verify the TFS aiming process, if desired.

Figure 28 *A functional/live handgun with a dry fire magazine inserted, a second dry fire magazine is shown alongside the handgun for reference*

At the time of writing, the optimal choice for dry fire training, TFS style, is the Mantis TitanX (see Figure 29). As tech progresses, I am sure other options will be available. This current choice is based on the enormous number of beneficial features and an exceptional level of safety. It's offered in various models, allowing the end user to match their training tool to their operational firearm. It is completely inert, eliminating any possibility of introducing live ammunition into it. A range of technology built into the unit can track movement, speed, trigger manipulation, and reaction time; it serves as a phenomenal data source for practical skills breakdown and assessment.

The TitanX has the option to project a laser from the muzzle. The visible laser can be on continually or flash momentarily when the trigger is pressed. The momentary flash as the trigger is pressed is the ultimate dry fire TFS test. If the laser is always on, the shooter can guide the muzzle where they want it. That might be a helpful training wheels approach, but unless they plan on having a laser on their live gun in the real world, it is not a transferable medium for aiming.

The laser that projects when the trigger is pressed provides real-time feedback for where the muzzle is pointed at that moment of 'firing'. This approach allows an actual test of the TFS aiming process. There is no indication of where the muzzle is pointed until you choose to test your aim. It is a tremendous opportunity for confidence and skill-building. The real feel of the pistol, coupled with its absolute safety, means it can be used to test the TFS approach in various environments. The laser will show on a projection screen or a TV. It will also indicate impact points on a walking, talking, moving human. This allows a dry fire and a safe approach to introducing real-world stimuli to the shooter. They can react and shoot – or not shoot – based on what they perceive versus being told what to shoot and when. This is an opportunity to interleave decision- making and assessment alongside motor skills.

Figure 29 *The Mantis TitanX is available in various models to replicate the real feel of a handgun and provide feedback in the form of an internal laser and analytical software*

This culmination of assessable accuracy while dry firing and the reality of being able to do it in any training environment is an exceptional training opportunity. The TitanX also has iron sights and the option to mount an optic. This allows for seamless transition of aiming technique, once more bridging the training and reality gap with versatility.

Dry-fire training is an underused skill-building opportunity. It's low cost, quiet and can be done almost anywhere and anytime. Whether you aim with the assistance of sights or not, dry-fire training with firearms is an enormous benefit to build comfort, efficiency, and automaticity in manipulation.

TFS and Iron Sights

It ain't what you don't know that gets you into trouble. It's what you know for sure that just ain't so.

- Mark Twain

At the time of writing this book, there are two broad categories that pistol sights fall into: iron sights and optics. Defining these two aiming systems involves another minefield of preferred terminology and unnecessary emotions. Optics are often referred to as red dots, although they are not all red and not all dots. Iron sights come in all kinds of shapes, colors, and materials, but are rarely made of iron. I will refer to them as iron sights and optics. If those terms are not what you use, feel free to translate them in your head to whatever works for you.

Pistol optics, when used correctly, are already a TFS tool. If you have the time and need for a sighted confirmation of your aiming process, the optic should not require any change in what you are visually focused on. There is a growing number of texts on the use of pistol optics. My intention is not to blur the focus of this book by making it about how to aim with an optic. The Cliff Notes version is this - put the 'dot' where the bullet needs to go and move the trigger without moving the gun. As long as you remain target-focused when, and if, you need the optic, you are doing it right.

I will spend the rest of this section on how iron sight use relates to this process. It is the most complex aiming process to translate to a TFS mindset. That translation is not complex because it is not conducive to the idea; it is complex due to the dogma surrounding the current teaching of iron sight use. I must challenge tradition, which may hurt the feelings of people emotionally attached to what they currently know. The classic image of an iron sight target alignment looks like Figure 30.

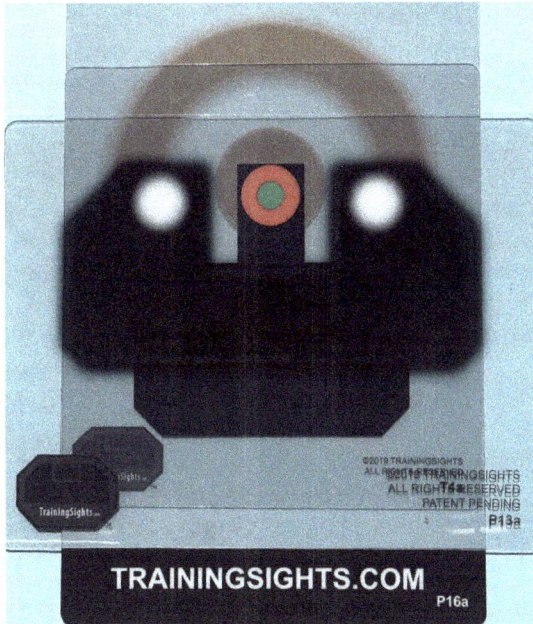

Figure 30 Image showing sight overlays with a blurred target, a clear focus on the front sight and blurred rear sight; demonstrating the common advice for visual focus when aiming a handgun. Overlays are from Trainingsights.com

If the assigned task is target shooting in a closed skill, zero-threat environment, nothing is wrong with this. Accompanied by an appropriate trigger press, this will be a reliable approach to aiming the handgun. General target shooting, plinking, or any recreational or non-time-compressed, low- or no-consequence event can be accomplished with this approach. It is not wrong. There are two changes I would offer when the use circumstances are fighting distance and fighting speed.

The first should not come as a shock at this point. I suggest being target-focused rather than sight-focused (see Figure 31). If you want or need to use iron sights, they will work even if the sights are blurred and the target is in focus. All other traditional elements of using the sights remain in place. The shooter should still begin target-focused, before the gun is drawn or presented from a ready position. The gun should be brought to eye level once looking toward what they intend to shoot. Essentially, the gun should interrupt the line of sight from the shooter's dominant eye to the target. The sights will be placed and aligned between the eye and the target. In an ideal world, it would look like Figure 31. Of course, the difference will be movement. The shooter's sights will never (yes, I said never) look like the picture unless the gun is in a vice. There will always be some movement.

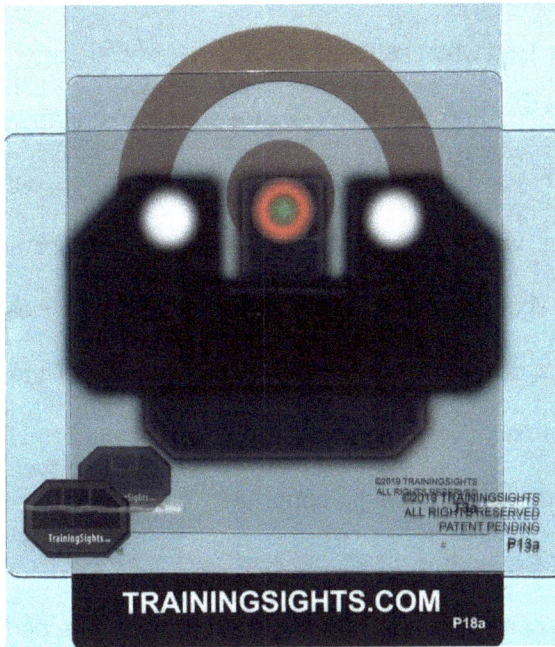

Figure 31 *Image showing sight overlays with clear focus on the target, and blurred front and rear sight; demonstrating the ability to attain sight alignment/picture while remaining target focused. Overlays are from Trainingsights.com*

One of the flaws in traditional law enforcement training is the pursuit of perfection regarding alignment of the sights. A brief clarification is in order regarding the word alignment. When I use it, I do not mean the alignment of the front and rear sights with one another. That is permanent. The front and rear sights are fixed in place when correctly and securely fastened. They remain aligned with one another permanently. What changes is the orientation of those sights in relation to our eye and the target. That is what we are aligning.

Now, back to alignment and what I like to call a good enough approach. Some of you baulked when you read the words 'good enough'. To some of you, that sounds shoddy and the hallmark of a suboptimal standard of work. You might be right if you hired a carpenter whose work was described as good enough. No one wants a door that drags along the floor and needs to be slammed shut. That is not the kind of good enough I am describing. Hiring a carpenter to board up a broken window in the middle of the night is a good enough solution to your immediate problem. When the sun comes up and businesses open, you will have the opportunity and resources for a more perfect solution, like a new window.

The sighting comparison for the opportunity to pursue perfection might be time, distance, and cover availability. That could allow the shooter to go prone and get maximum protection, comfort and stability. The circumstances for good enough might be the need to make a hit, or hits much closer, without the availability of cover or much time. If a would-be murderer is charging an officer in an alleyway with a few yards between them, a 'good enough' application of sights might be all that is needed.

Good enough sights are another learned skill. From the very first days of sight use, instructors need to go beyond using static visuals—like pictures, sketches, or PowerPoints—that merely illustrate equal light and height. I like a visual, movable representation of sights. It allows the demonstration of sight overlay on whatever will be shot. The best and most diverse visual aids for this purpose come from TrainingSights. Their website has just about every conceivable sight variance. The individual graphics can be overlaid on one another and moved independently. This allows for movement to be shown like the constant wobble whenever a human holds a handgun, right up to the extreme of what happens when someone introduces a colossal level of movement into the gun. This type of trigger ATTACK causes people to miss entire score zones as they attempt to 'capture' the perfect sight picture. The trigger attack isn't an iron sight issue specifically; optic users do it, too.

An impactful way to show how bad sight alignment can be is to shoot a demo with intentionally misaligned sights. This blew my mind when I first saw it; it continues to blow the minds of experienced shooters and instructors today. The demo starts at fifteen feet. The version for the book is shot on an 8-inch circle. Eight inches does not hold any mystical relevance. This can be done on any target. I choose an 8-inch circle as it is somewhat of an industry standard, and it is typically easy for people to relate to what they see here. The demo comes in five stages.

Stage 1: Align the sights as usual and shoot the center of the score zone (see Figure 32).

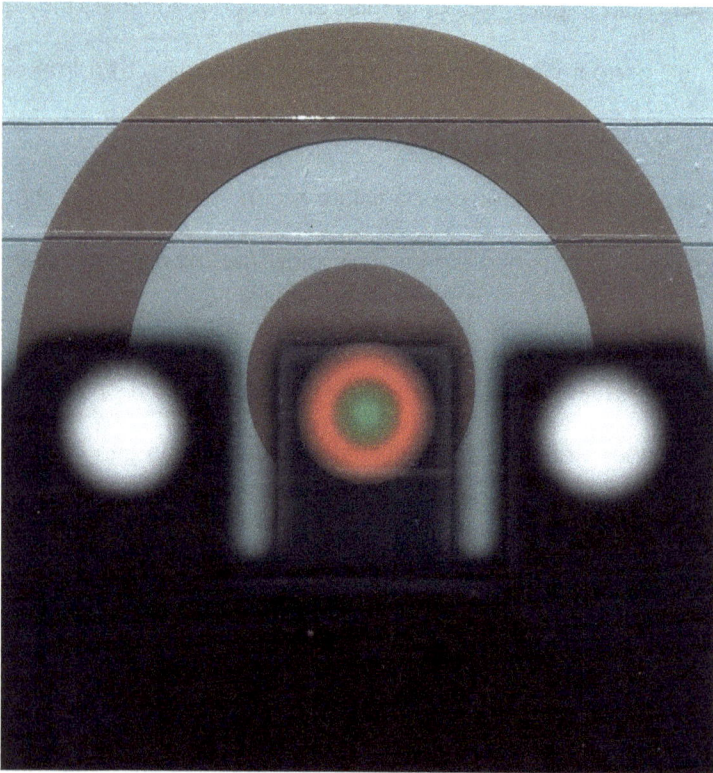

Figure 32 *Image showing sight overlays with clear focus on the target, and blurred front and rear sights; demonstrating the ability to attain sight alignment/picture while remaining target focused. Overlays are from Trainingsights.com*

Stage 2: Show the front sight moved significantly to the left. I do this with the visual aid. Show them what the alignment will look like and ask them to guess how far over the bullet impact will be. This is another example of the power of questions as a training tool. It allows you to assess what the shooters know or believe to be true. The guesses will range dramatically, but it is good to understand the group's expectations. You will learn what misconceptions they may have, and what they have been doing to aim to this point.

Figure 33 Image showing sight overlays with clear focus on the target, and blurred front and rear sights; this offset shows the consequence of the front sight being extremely misaligned to the left. Overlays are from Trainingsights.com

Stage 3: Mirroring the previous stage, the front sight is driven to the right side (see Figure 34).

Figure 34 Image showing sight overlays with clear focus on the target, and blurred front and rear sights; this offset shows the consequence of the front sight being extremely misaligned to the right. Overlays are from Trainingsights.com

Stage 4: With the left and right limits explored, some preconceived ideas will already be destroyed. Stages 4 and 5 deal with elevation. These may now be less earth-shattering and perhaps a little more expected. I still show the shooters with the visual aids what I will be doing with the sights and ask them for their expectations of deviation from the initial point of aim. For this stage, I lower the front sight almost to the point of disappearing (see Figure 35).

Figure 35 Image showing sight overlays with clear focus on the target, and blurred front and rear sights; this offset shows the consequence of the front sight being extremely misaligned, centered but low. Overlays are from Trainingsights.com

Stage 5: Mirroring the previous stage, the front sight is driven high. Sitting at about twice its normal height (see Figure 36).

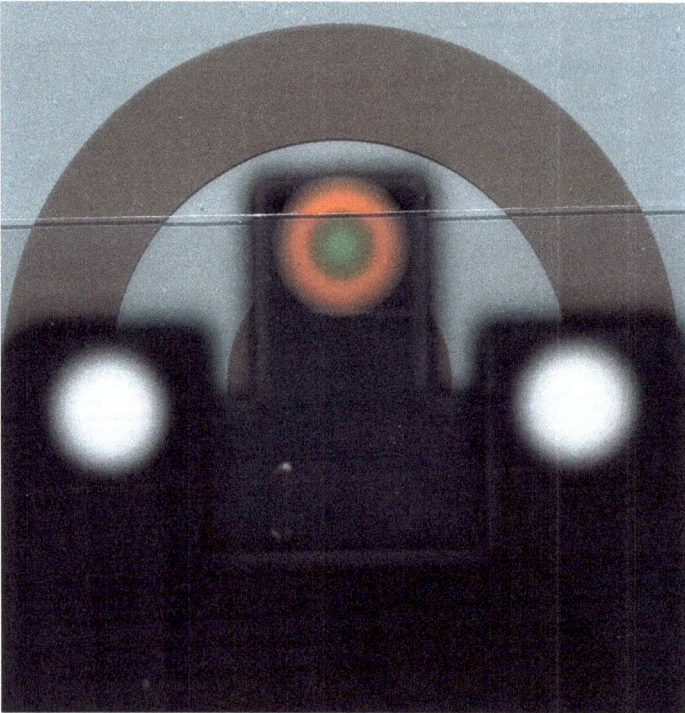

Figure 36 Image showing sight overlays with clear focus on the target, and blurred front and rear sights; this offset shows the consequence of the front sight being extremely misaligned, centered but high. Overlays are from Trainingsights.com

The result of the demonstration is shown in Figure 37.

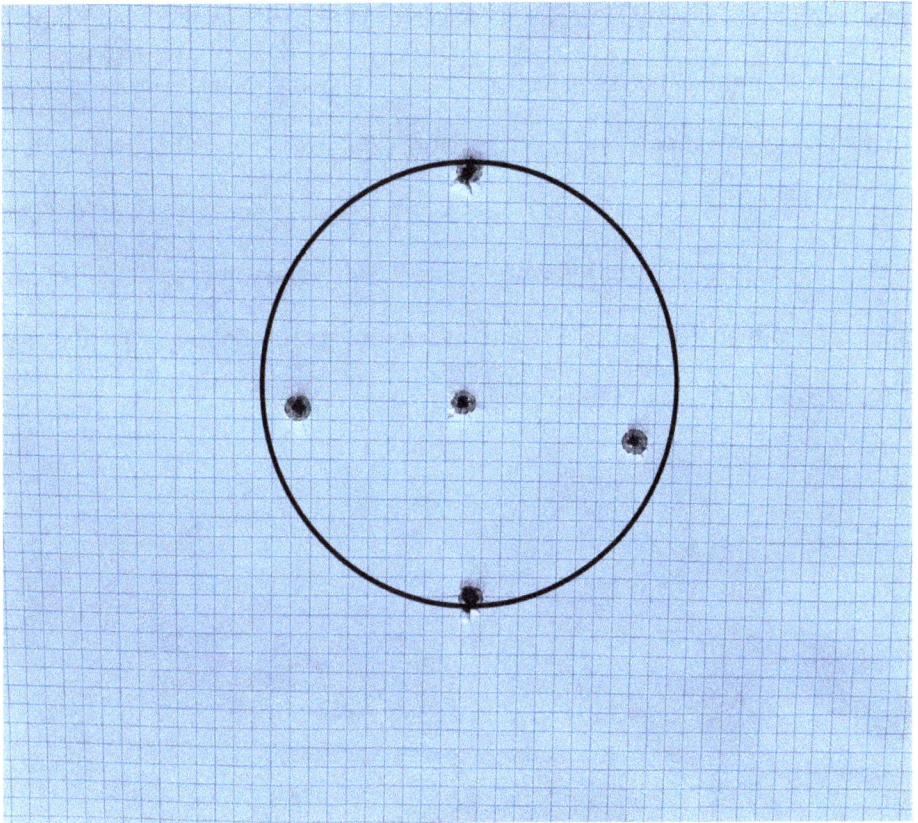

Figure 37 *Image shows the outcome of the handgun being shot with the misaligned sights shown in stage 1-5 of the preceding drill*

The extremes will create a diamond-shaped style. Based on this gun, at this distance, with these sights, the extremes of sight misalignment produce this result. Varying the distance from the target, the gun, and the sights will produce minor variances in the extremes. You will still get the diamond shape, but a thinner front sight and a narrower rear sight notch mean the gun will be moved by less of an angle left to right. If the gun has a taller front sight and a deeper rear notch, a greater angle of deviation will result from the up and down shots.

When the shooter has seen just how bad the alignment can be in comparison to the textbook imagery they were probably exposed to when they first learned how to use sights, it should open the door for discussion about good enough sights. Any of the variances shown in Figure 38 would be within the 8-inch circle, shot from fifteen feet away. They would all be good enough to hit that set standard of accuracy with an appropriate trigger press.

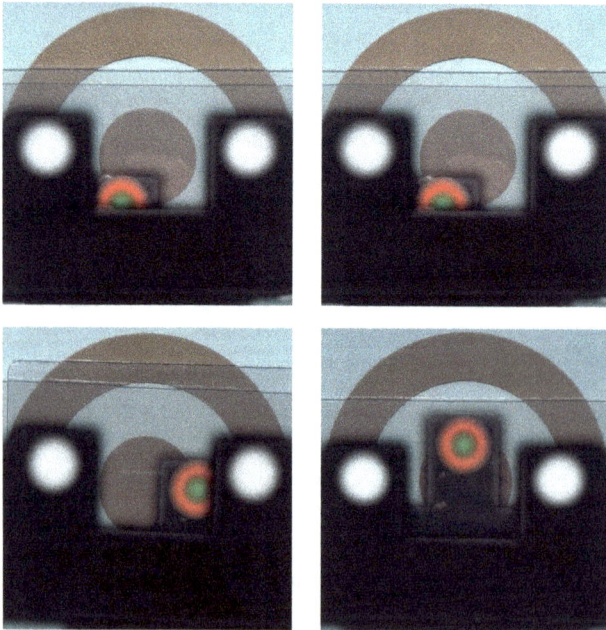

Figure 38 *Image showing sight overlays with clear focus on the target, and blurred front and rear sights; each of the four variations of misaligned handgun sights would create a hit inside the extremes shown in Figure 37. Overlays are from Trainingsights.com*

The takeaway from this exercise is if a shooter wants or needs sights to make a hit, they can still be target-focused, and they can still be fast. Transitioning focus to the front sight and waiting for perfection in alignment is unnecessary. This understanding of what their sights need to look like to hit their target is an often-overlooked area of training that can open the door for new levels of speed and accuracy.

Understanding their gun and their limitations goes hand in hand with this. If the shooter is at 75 feet trying to hit something 6 inches in diameter, one of the extremes used in the demonstration will not be good enough. The shooter will miss the intended target. One of the ways to show the limitation of this is through shooters experimenting with the drill themselves. There are two live fire versions recommended. If you have the time and the resources, run both in succession the first time you introduce this concept. For continuation or in-service training of people familiar with the basic principle, I move right to drill two.

Drill one

Start close and work backward incrementally. Use whatever target or score zone you define as acceptable. Run this with no time limit.

2 yards: Shoot the extremes of the sight alignment drill, mirroring the demo discussed previously in this section. They will start with the standard sight alignment and then deviate left, right, up, and down in their own time. Once it is safe to do so, move forward and require them to draw out the diamond—label

it with the distance it was created at (see Figure 39).

Repeat the drill at 4, 6, 8 yards, etc.

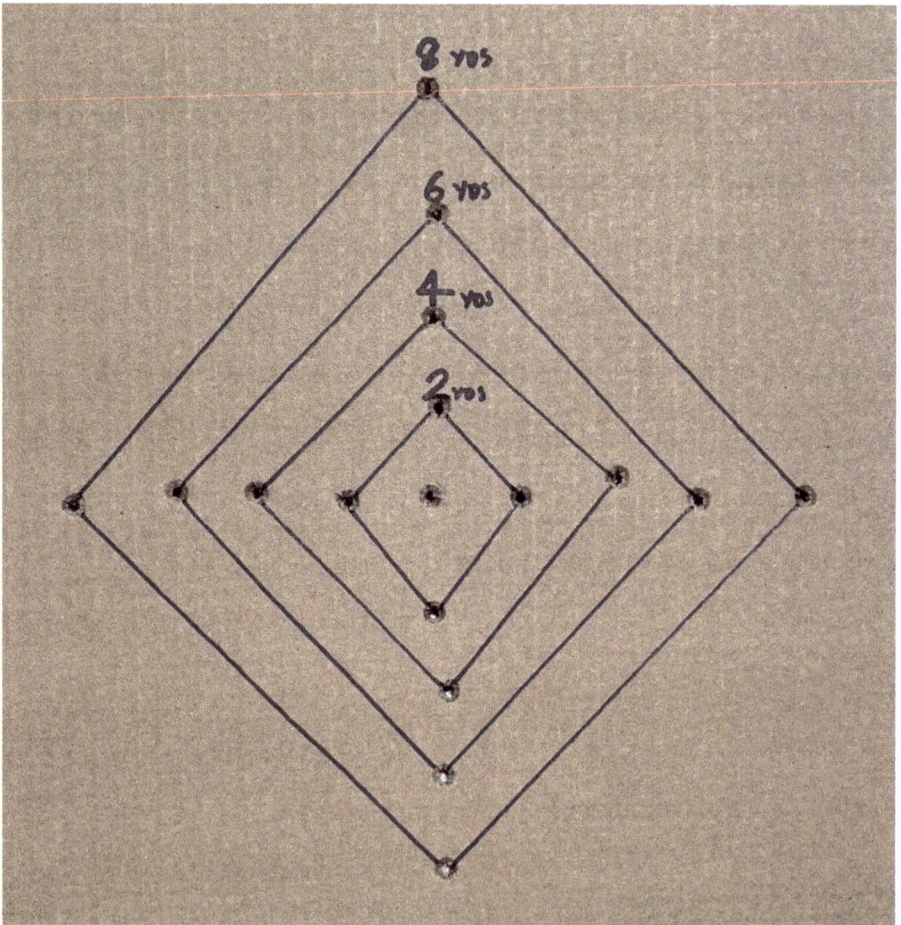

Figure 39 *Image of a target showing results from a shooter using the examples of sight misalignment. The drill was shot at 2,4,6 and 8 yards. As the shooter increases their distance from the target, the shot group grows incrementally larger*

Continue until the diamonds produced are entirely outside the score zone you deemed acceptable (see Figure 40). This allows some individual discovery with the good enough concept. Shooters may have different guns, different slide lengths, different sights, and, most importantly, different skill sets!

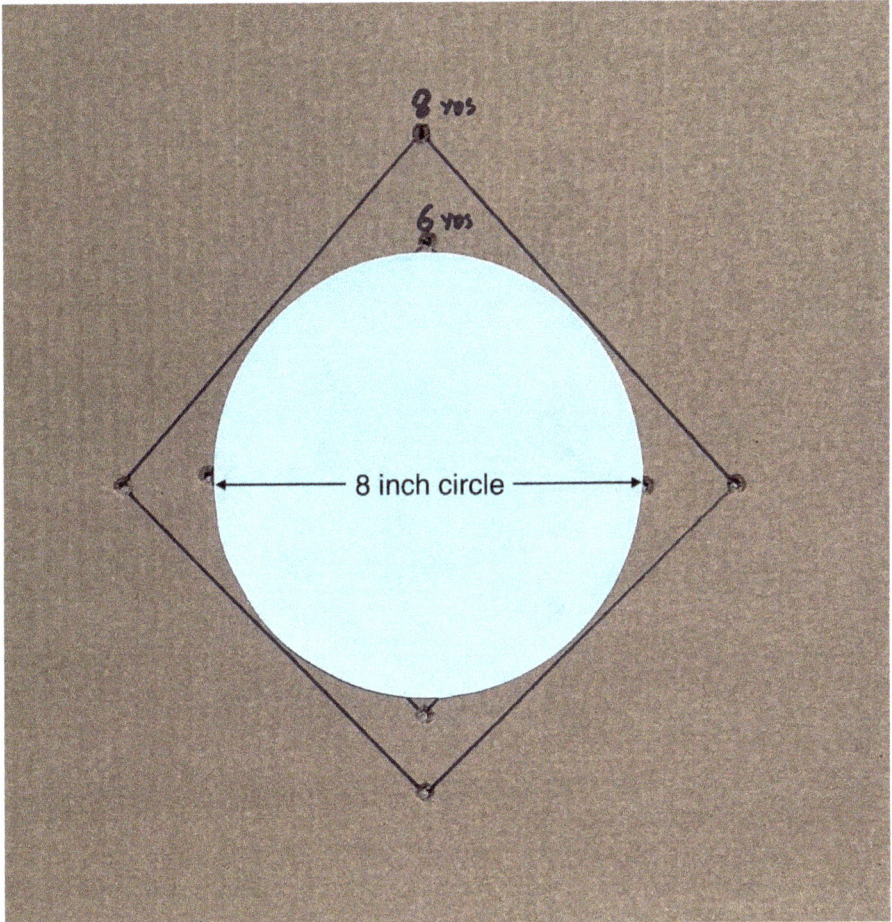

Figure 40 *Image of figure 39 with the addition of an 8-inch circle for size reference*

The theory of this process is one thing, but the application makes it an excellent area for individualized learning. If the shooter has, for example, a tendency to drive their shots low and left, this will affect the positions of their diamonds (see Figure 41).

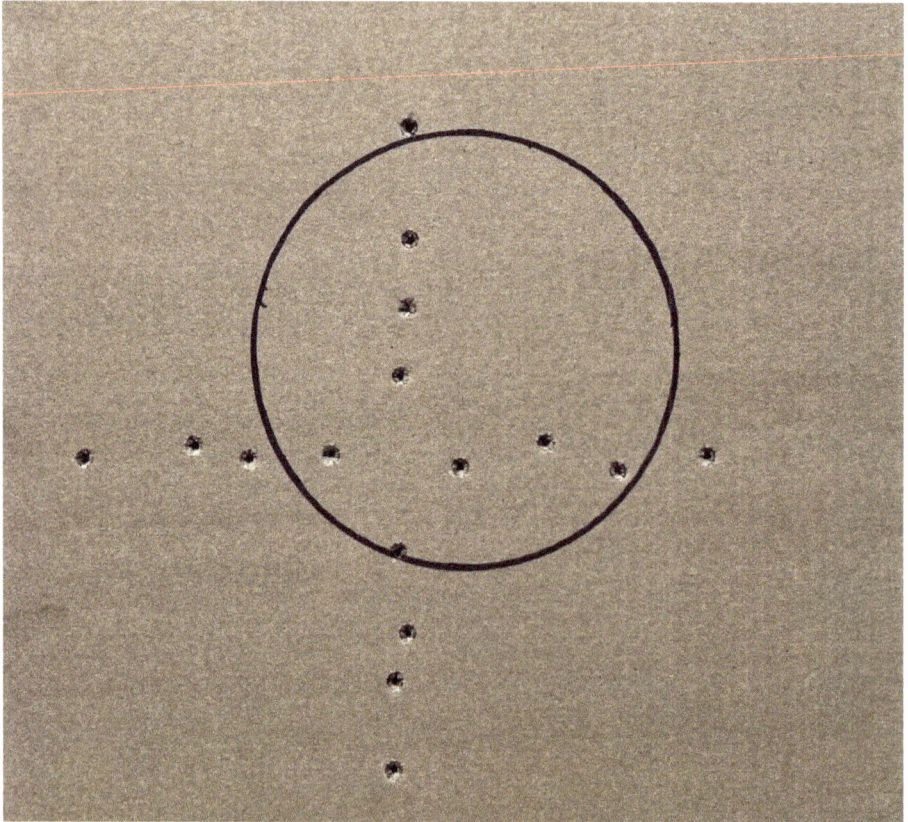

Figure 41 *Image of a target showing results from an inaccurate shooter using the examples of sight misalignment from figures 32-36. The drill was shot at 2,4,6 and 8 yards. As the shooter increases their distance from the target, the shot group grows incrementally larger. The shooters tendency to move the gun shows the consequence of misaligned sights and suboptimal technique combined.*

I am not suggesting Figure 41 is an acceptable end state. There is a fundamental developmental issue for this shooter, and that must be addressed. A great many law enforcement shooters have things they need to improve. They will not all be able to create the perfect diamond on demand, even in a closed skill, low-stress, untimed environment. This drill applies to what a good enough sight picture looks like, and what an individual shooter can expect as their outcome when combining sight misalignment with their current skill set. That leads us to the next drill.

Drill 2

Once again, this should ideally start close. The acceptable level of accuracy is for you, as the coach to define. For simplicity, this example will maintain the 8-inch circle, it's preferable to use a negative target, completely removing the defined score zone (see Figure 42). The negative target is a wonderful way to break the habit of the one-hole perfectionists. With a negative target, any 'hit' that was good enough will leave the target unscathed. There is literally nothing to see. The negative target can be a great confidence builder for good enough hits. Anything in the score zone is as valuable as anything else in the score zone.

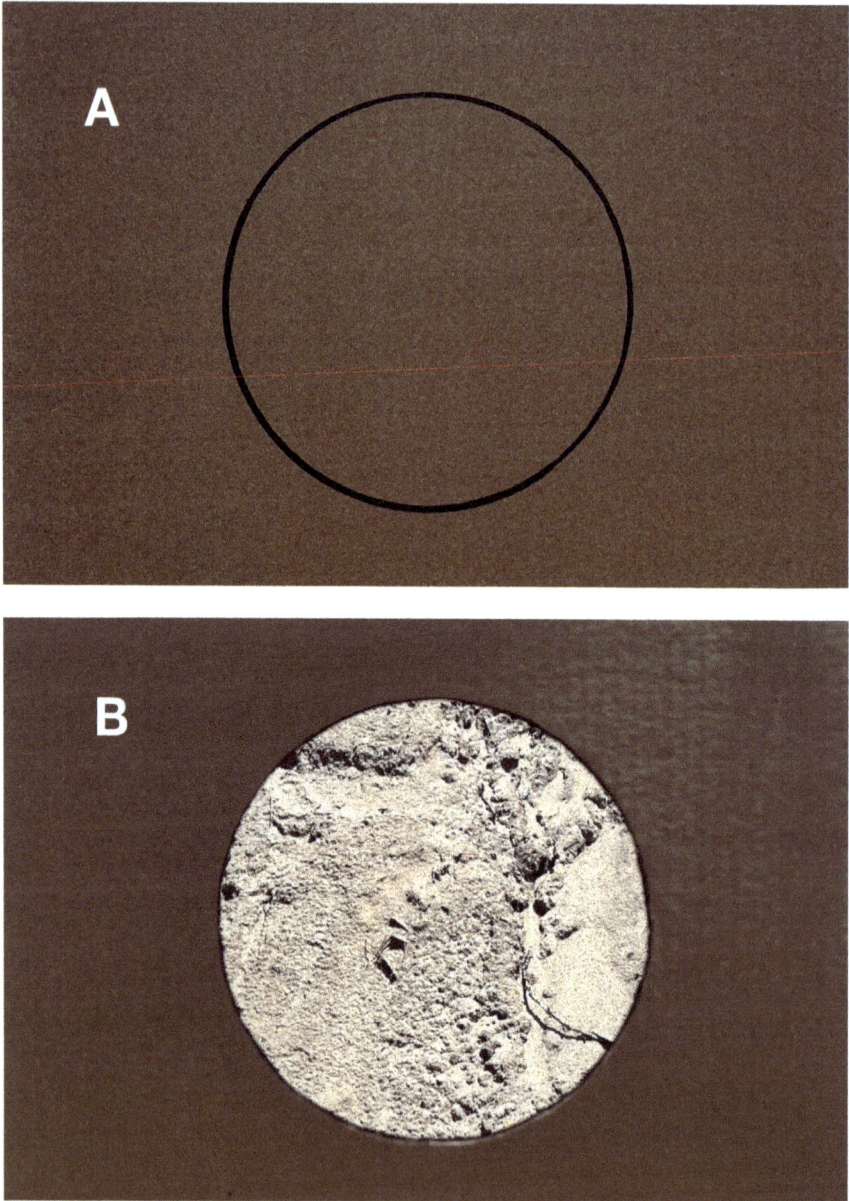

Figure 42 *Image of two examples with an 8-inch defined target area. One is defined with a circle outline (A), the other is defined by removing the acceptable score zone (B). The 'negative' target remains unshot if the shooter is acceptably accurate*

2 Yards: Allow the shooter to explore incrementally the misalignment of their sights in a more freestyle manner. They no longer have to start at the center. They no longer must stick to the rigidity of the straight up and down or just left to right movement; they can play with variances of misalignment. The outcome is shown in Figure 43.

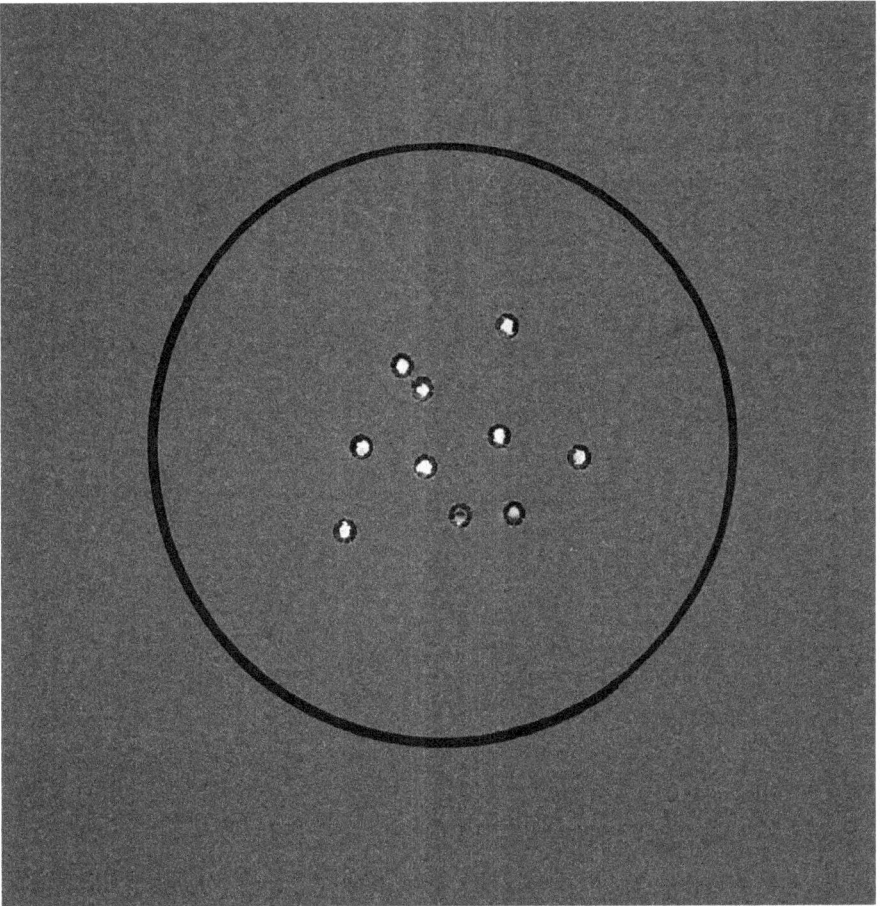

Figure 43 Image of a target showing results from a shooter intentionally misaligning their sights, like the examples shown in Figure 38

This should all be target-focused. If the negative target is your preference, the shooter can be looking through it. Assign a round count if you must, or better still, a window of rounds to keep practice varied. You could, for example, tell your shooters to fire somewhere between 10 and 15 rounds. Their objective is to experiment with sight misalignment while keeping the rounds inside the score zone. If a round or two goes outside, that is ok. That is a learning opportunity. If they cannot keep any hits inside the designated zone, that problem must be diagnosed and treated.

Once they have found their comfort zone at that distance, repair or replace the target. Note: marking the misses for this drill with a pen and leaving the holes visible can become confusing for the learning objective. Each iteration should be a clean target. Every 'miss' should be something the shooter can associate with a visual reference of sights.

Work the shooters backward incrementally, 4, 6, 8 yards, etc. The art of coaching comes into play in how far back you go and how much ammunition you use at each stage. The overall takeaway should allow shooters to understand what they need to see, depending on where they are, to make the hits that the task requires. Although this drill should be a discovery learning moment, it is not the end of the process. As with all things, it cannot be a one-and-done event. Once there is a basic appreciation for what can be done, on a static range and a static target, it is time to add variation and complexity. The

Training TFS

goal is to be able to use this aiming technique with opposition. Knowing how to do it on the range is just the starting point.

TFS should not be limited to a narrow window of use in obscure or imagined circumstances. TFS must integrate with every other aspect of firearms training. It is possible to stay target-focused and aim a handgun without using sights, as well as while using iron sights, or an optic. What drives the aiming process is the availability of time and distance. The more time and distance you have, the more refined the aiming process can, and should be.

TFS Attention Drill

Those who were taken by surprise tended not to see their sights and looked at the threat.

- Mroz, 2000

Getting overly committed to a task can be detrimental. If we find ourselves buried in a notebook, reading on a scene, or immersed in a laptop while sitting in a parking lot, we risk exposing ourselves to unseen danger. If our top-down attentional task becomes so immersive that we become inattentively blind to our surroundings, we have a problem brewing.

Our sensory systems monitor the background to keep us safe. A commonly experienced example of the sensory background processing is sometimes called the cocktail party phenomenon (Cherry, 1953). Although you do not have to be at a cocktail party to relate (I have never been to an actual cocktail party). You may have had this experience if you have been in a crowded room, or a busy restaurant. While you are busy waxing lyrical and being a fantastic conversationalist, there are many other conversations taking place. There is an abundance of background noise. Yet you filter all of that from your conscious mind and focus on the discussion you are having. Those other noises and conversations are not invisible or hidden, if you were to hear your name being spoken by someone else nearby you will pick up on that cue. You were not attending to that conversation, but when your name was spoken you noticed. Upon hearing your name, the part of your brain dutifully monitoring the background for relevance pushed through your top-down task. Like a puppy bringing you her favorite toy, your brain bounced into your conversation and said, "Hey, do you need this?"

That background monitoring process is helpful for threat awareness, too. It also happens with our other senses; it is not just an auditory phenomenon. These background monitoring processes are essential to our survival. When we needed to be out hunting for our food, we also had to be peripherally aware that something else could be hunting us simultaneously.

If we become too wrapped up in a narrow task, we risk sliding into inattentional blindness and missing all these cues. Have you ever found yourself staring at someone who has just finished speaking to you. They are looking at you expectantly as if they are awaiting a response. You have no idea what they were saying. Many a relationship breakdown has begun this way! This experience would be the opposite of the cocktail party effect. You were physically present and supposedly involved in the conversation but heard nothing.

These experiences of attentional resource management are not closed skill realm events. The environment in which we train should include exposure to this. Managing attentional resources and experiencing bottom-up interruptions and stimuli to the top-down world are essential. If we are funneled into working on a live fire range, there are ways we can begin to vary our training beyond just a static and predetermined aiming point.

The attention drill is a fun and straightforward game you can play on a range to keep attentional focus broader than concentrating narrowly on a static bullet hole. It is a little ammo heavy, but it is a fast and fun way to show and practice the skill of keeping attention external and broad. It is a building block to a more varied and higher-fidelity training realm.

Attention Drill

This drill requires two shooters sharing one target. Use a blank backer/plain paper for the first iteration and stage the shooters 9 – 12 feet from the target. Shooter A begins by firing a shot randomly anywhere on the target (see Figure 44).

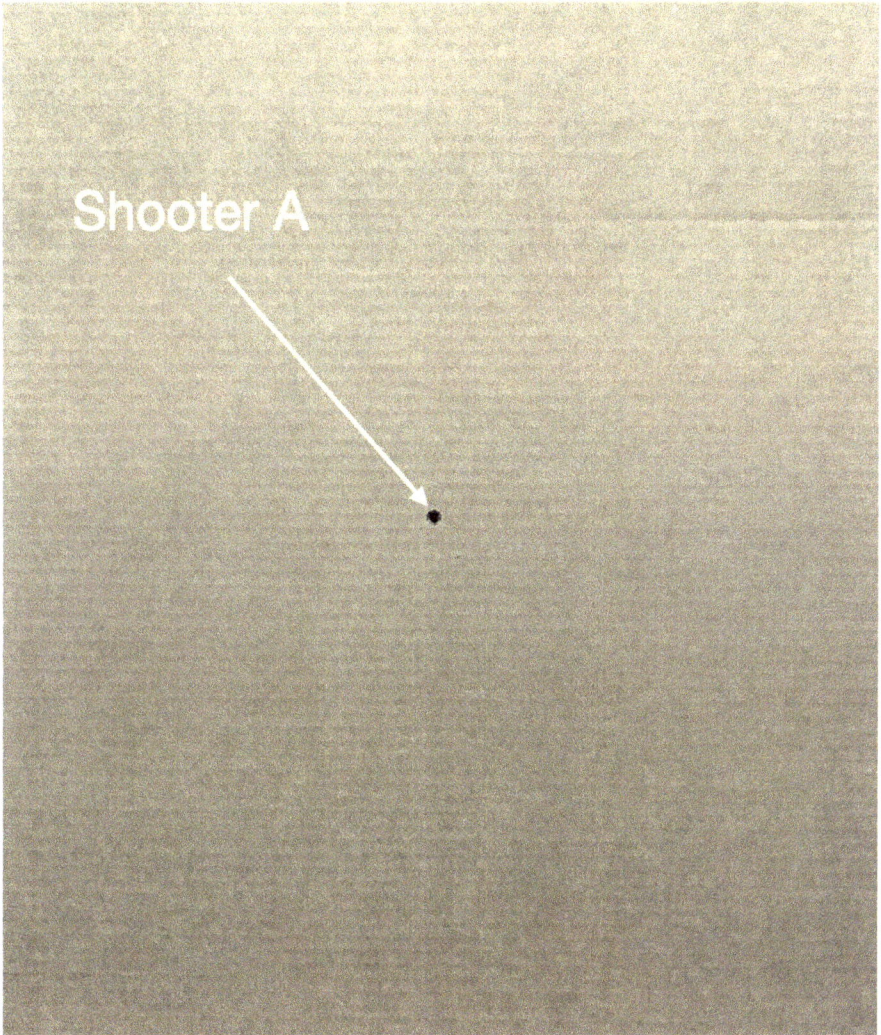

Figure 44 *Image of a target with a single bullet hole fired by 'Shooter A'*

Shooter B identifies the hole created by that shot. That hole now becomes their

target. They are allowed to fire one round to attempt to hit it (see Figure 45).

255

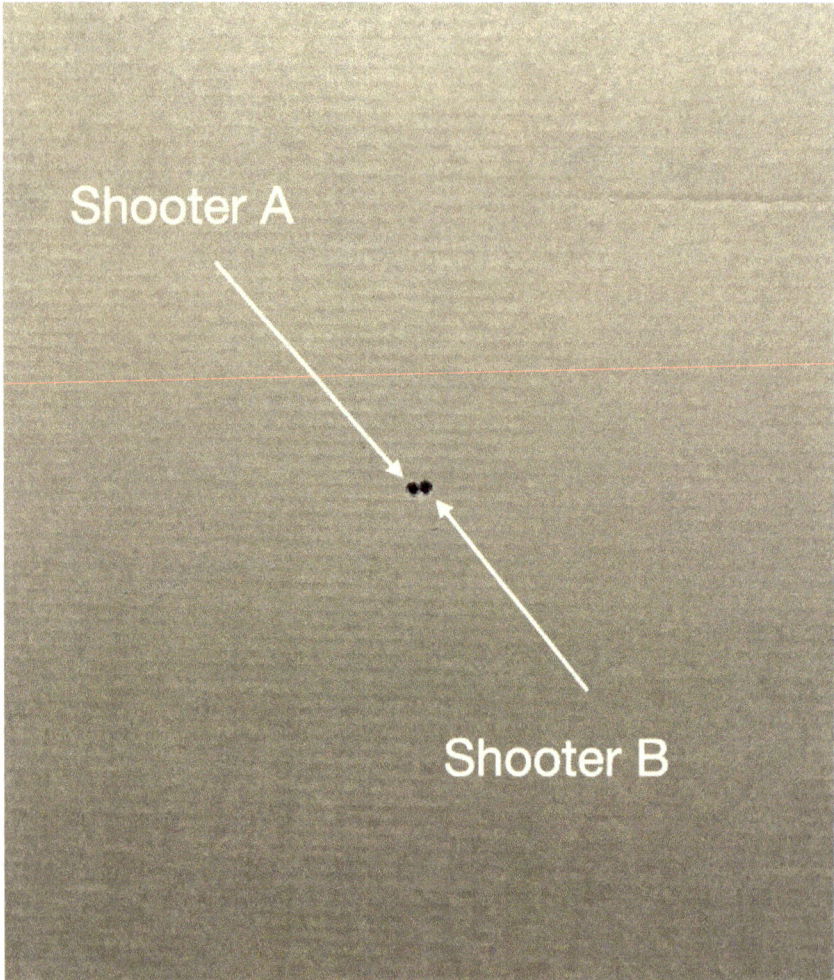

Figure 45 *Image of a target with one bullet hole, created by 'Shooter A' which was the target, and a second bullet hole created by the shot from 'Shooter B'*

Immediately upon Shooter B engaging the bullet hole, Shooter A fires another shot with random placement on the target. That now becomes Shooter B's new target, and they must fire a round and try to hit it (see Figure 46).

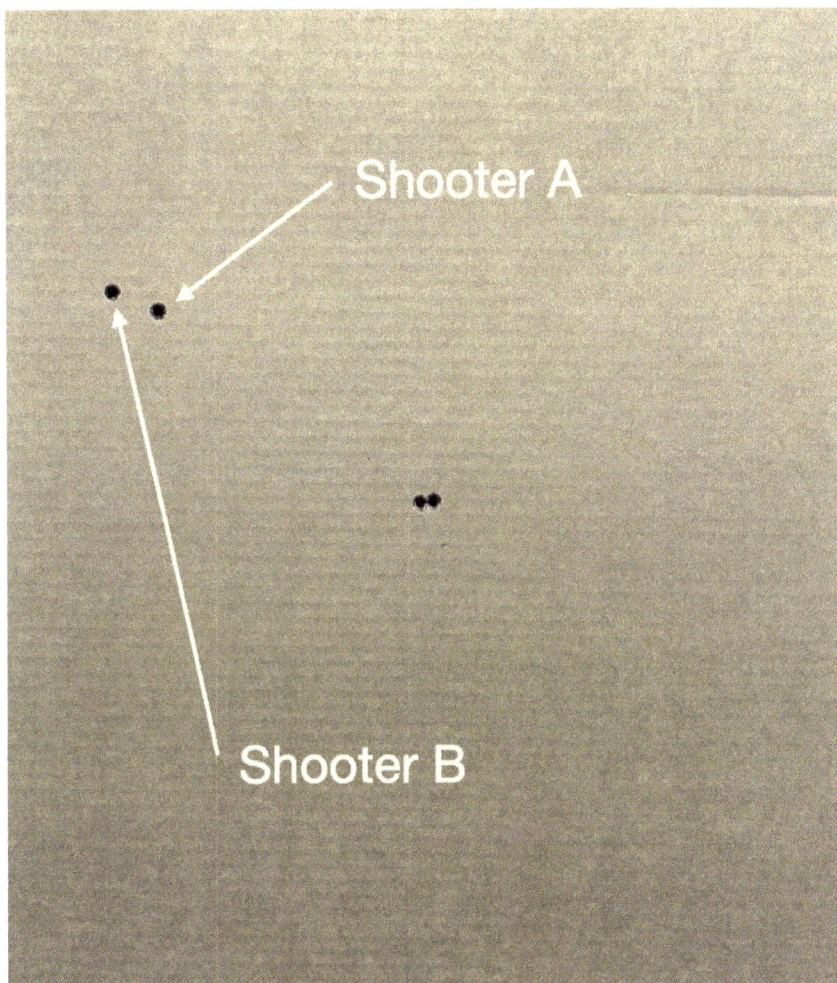

Figure 46 Image of a target with a 'new' bullet hole, created by 'Shooter A' which was the target, and a second bullet hole created by the shot from 'Shooter B'

The drill repeats until the allocated round count is met (see Figure 47). I usually make the round count one complete magazine. Adjust as your ammunition budget allows. When the shooters reload, the drill is complete. They swap roles and then repeat the task.

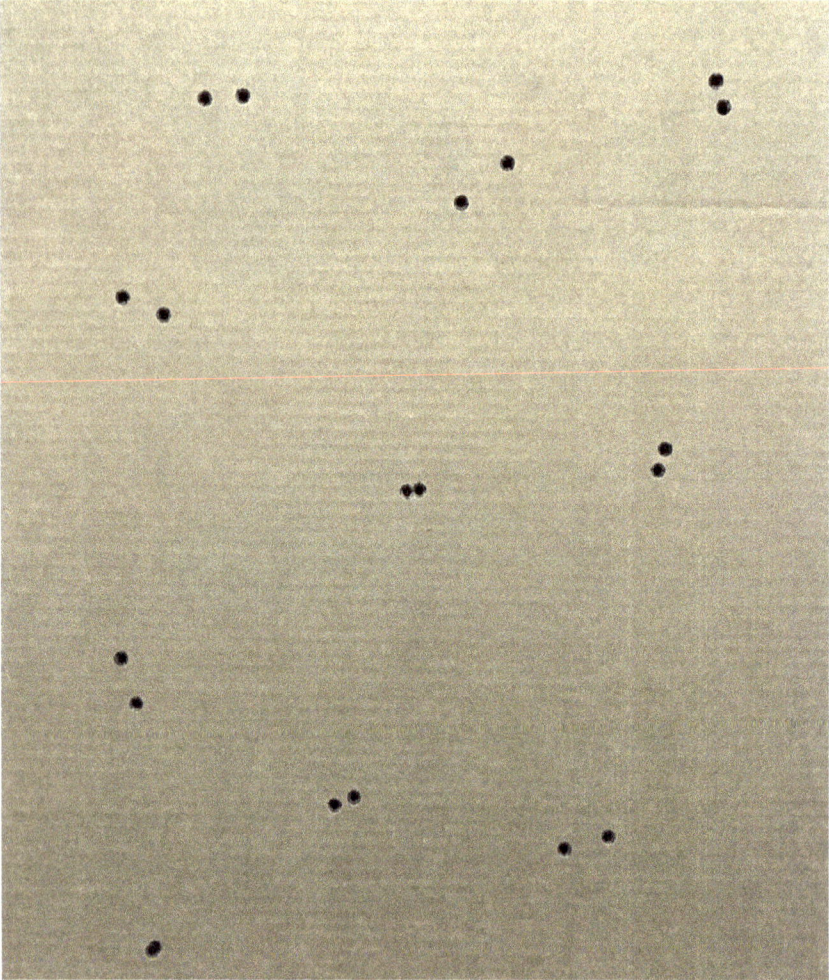

Figure 47 *Image of a target where two shooters completed ten repetitions of the attention drill*

Variations to the Attention Drill

The basic drill can be challenging enough on its own. However, a few ways exist to vary it and increase its complexity to keep your shooters challenged.

Desirable difficulty and contextual interference are strategic tools to tailor the task and keep your learners on the cusp of their comfort zone.

- Increase the distance

- Use a target repeatedly so it becomes distractingly full of holes

- Use a target with other designs

- Complete it in low, altered, or failing light

- Use multiple paper targets

- Use multiple steel targets

- Work the drill from ready positions or holsters

- Make it a shoot/no shoot response based on the shot placement

- Add inert training rounds to the magazines to induce malfunctions, compelling attentional shift, and grip breakdown/reestablishment

- Require movement before, during or after the shots are taken

The list could go on. The key takeaway is that you should not get narrowly stuck in training one skill one way. Blend skills. Keep the training varied and challenging. The attention drill demands that shooters focus during the entire shooting sequence. It helps them to build on their understanding of the relationship between visual stability and shooting accuracy. Remember, this is a building block to high-fidelity open skill training and real-world application.

TFS as a Diagnostic Tool

Do the best you can until you know better. Then, when you know better, do better.

- Maya Angelou

Shooting without using sights can be an eye-opening moment for other reasons. Some of the most violent deviations from hitting what they intend to come from shooters trying to capture the moment when their sighting system is directed at what they want to hit. They <u>attack</u> the trigger, moving their whole hand and both arms, and some throw their back and shoulder muscles into the movement, too.

This over-exuberant attempt to make the gun fire the instant they point it where they want ironically causes them to miss dramatically. It is common to see someone using sights miss by 18 to 24 inches while standing stationary 5 yards away from their static target. Often, the shooter does not know they are doing it; they do not have any idea how much they are moving the gun. There are several approaches to show them what they are doing, and various ways coaches like to break the cycle of self-defeat. Taking away the sights is my preferred approach.

If they shoot with their vision and attention on the target, there is no timing of sight use. The stimulus that usually drives the full-body attack on the trigger is eliminated, and their ability to hit what they intend to increases dramatically. Often, shooters who miss dramatically will see improved results immediately with a target-focused approach compared to what they achieved with sight use.

The art of coaching comes into play regarding how long you stay target-focused before reintroducing sights. Each shooter is on a different path, with different levels of experience and learning to undertake. This approach serves as a great diagnostic and can provide the shooter with that 'ah-ha' moment when they see how their physical input is affecting the shot placement and outcome.

Get Off the Range!

1835

I repeat what on a former occasion I maintained, namely, that "practice to be useful should take place in the situation, and in THE VERY manner, in which the acquired improvement is likely to be called into action."

(Lt Col Baron De Berenger, 1835)

1942

Practice under circumstances which approximate as nearly as possible to actual fighting conditions.

(Fairbairn et al., 1942)

2000

Again, if instructors really want to teach survival skills, they must introduce the elements of surprise, movement, uneven terrain, startle, and human opponents into their students' training.

(Mroz, 2000)

2022

Training should also include appropriate amounts of representative practice that is commensurate with real-world settings.

(Baldwin et al., 2022)

The message has been clear for a long time. Yet somehow, law enforcement trainers and administrators seem to find a way to pretend it hasn't been said. There is merit to shooting on a live-fire range. Don't misinterpret my message; I encourage you to do it as often as you can. However, the transferable skills that can be built regarding decision-making and adaptability are limited within that same environment.

Shooting on a square range is a closed skill, with predictable targets and controlled conditions. Variability is usually minimized, and trainees focus on perfecting the technical aspects of performance. This is often misconstrued as all that is essential for developing basic firearms proficiency. However, while these skills might check a box in training, they do not replicate the dynamic challenges officers face during real-world incidents. Building solid, transferable skill sets and experience with operating live guns is critical. That training must also be focused on the user's end goal. Training in the environmental context where the skill will be called into action is an essential progression. The closer you get the training environment and stimuli to match the operational environment, the more prepared your people will be.

To maximize the effectiveness of training programs, a substantial portion of training time must be dedicated to open skill scenarios. This approach ensures that officers are well-versed in technical skills and adept at applying these skills in real-world situations. Furthermore, open skill training should begin early and progressively escalate in complexity to promote integrated skill development and retention. There is a significant difference between the expectation and the reaction of standing on a range, waiting for a target to turn, and talking to another human being who suddenly reaches into their waistband.

Creating opportunities for people to learn the visual cues that initiate a response in the real world is powerful and essential. The novice vs. expert study in the research chapter (Vickers & Lewinski, 2012) is an example of how experience matters when it comes to knowing where to look. Officers with years of experience see things differently. They have learned, through practice and sometimes through errors and failures, what is important NOW. High-performing officers consistently demonstrate superior ability to identify and process task-relevant information. This skill goes beyond mere observation – it is about knowing:

- Where to look for critical information
- How to filter out non-essential data
- When to shift attention based on evolving situations

Attentional direction and prioritization skills can be learned and developed. That learning can begin as early as the academy's introduction to firearms and continue through in-service training over a whole career. Diversification of the training environment, both in respect of terrain, stimuli, and interaction with both, has a huge number of benefits. Here are a few examples to help clarify the gaps I am referring to. The list is not exhaustive, but hopefully it gets you thinking in the right direction.

The Turning Target Problem

Skills training should primarily be focused on preparing people with a relevant response to an expected and relevant stimulus. Turning targets or audible cues do not replicate that.

In civilian life, we teach people to drive cars on public roads, not so they can be exposed to every conceivable circumstance, but so they have essential skills to navigate comparable ones. They know what it is like to maneuver around other cars and people. They begin learning to 'read the road' and anticipate what other drivers will do before they do it. I feel like a psychic most days on the highway as I predict the lane-chopping and changing I am about to witness; even though no one uses their turn signal, I can predict what's coming based on countless prior events banked as learned visual cues.

Someone who learned to drive a car on a closed track built of cones may be able to start, stop, and turn a corner, but they will not have the tacit knowledge to predict an unsignaled lane change. A track-trained driver is not ready to negotiate a Florida Highway at rush hour during a thunderstorm. They have no idea how to interact with their ever-changing real environment. In the same way, if the only stimulus for drawing a gun has been a turning paper target or a verbal cue, we are not helping people associate their response with the real world. There is a disconnect between what they have been ingrained to do and what they are supposed to be preparing to do. Turning targets are fine; they have a use, but they cannot be the only stimulus ever used for firearms training. We must get people in front of people.

The movement problem

As I referenced earlier, a new requirement for a single sidestep while drawing was enough to unravel the illusion of skill possessed by seasoned police officers during their qualification. Their agency required them to shoot the qual, so they learned to do that. Even the slightest change of requirement within the closed skill realm uncovered the fragility of their limited skills. That failure occurred with explicit instruction and a static target. Now imagine if the target moved too, and there had been no instruction to follow. How would rigid test-taking ability work out as a response? I am not predicting well.

With that example in mind, we need movement. Lots and lots of movement. The officers need the freedom to move. With the proper organization, that can be done with live fire on a range, but we are still limiting the target options to inert surfaces when we use live guns, and that space. We need human subjects in contextually relevant surroundings and appropriate non-lethal training tools to replace live guns. Those human subjects the officers are engaging with will need the freedom to move. It does not have to be a vast or infinite landscape. Even if the training space is small, it can still be tremendously valuable. A single room gives people the opportunity to move in every direction. A single room also provides an interesting constraint. There is only so much distance you can create. So, running away is scratched from the list of options. Put some furniture in the environment and see how that changes interaction with the terrain.

Getting people able to move, turn, and potentially shoot in any direction is a step toward a more adaptable skill set. Whenever we can create the opportunity for the subject to be another human who can interact with the officer, we are working toward building a more robust transferable skill set.

Conclusion

Today's technology far exceeds what Fairbairn and Sykes had in Shanghai in the early 1900s. They found a way to make their training more realistic with rudimentary ingenuity. We are surrounded by resources and equipment to replicate real-world weapons, such as less-lethal ammunition and laser pistols. We can even simulate the real world with video and virtual reality. There is no excuse for not diversifying training; we must leap into it!

Law enforcement officers' effectiveness in critical situations depends heavily on the complex interplay of visual perception, cognitive processing, and physical response. Understanding and developing these relationships is crucial for optimal operational performance. The connection between perception and action in firearms handling is cyclical and dynamic. What officers see directly influences their decisions and responses, impacting what they need to perceive next. This continuous feedback loop forms the foundation of effective firearms operation in high-stress situations. It must be a part of their firearms training.

Effective firearms training for law enforcement must go beyond mechanical skill development (Cooper et al., 2024). Officers can develop more robust, adaptable operational capabilities by understanding and training in the relationship between perception, cognition, and action.

CHAPTER 12 - PARTING THOUGHTS

Be curious, not judgmental.

- Ted Lasso

Tradition is a Two-Sided Coin

Beautiful tradition

There are some places where tradition belongs. I get a frisson (goosebumps and a wonderful tingling sensation) when I see the flag raised and hear the Star-Spangled Banner sung with verve. I never want that to change. I wish that feeling could last forever.

Toxic tradition

Tradition can also destroy progress and culture. I recently heard a chief of police in a department decimated by recruitment and retention refuse to allow an officer to attend training. The officer was asking to train on their day off and pay for the course and the materials themselves. The chief only had to say yes. The chief said no. Why? Tradition—he never lets 'new' people go to training.

The officer had two decades of prior service and had been with that department for over a year. The chief was openly counting the days to his own retirement and seemed more interested in doing what he had always done, even though the department was falling into ruins around him. The chief's actions led to that officer leaving the department, but the commitment to his tradition remained solid.

When it comes to training, tradition kills progress. Doing what you have always done is not a good enough reason or a sufficient justification. Just because you trained that way and succeeded does not validate the process. Succeeding despite something is not the same as succeeding because of something. Training should be alive with change and a hunger for a better answer.

I was fortunate enough to spend many years leading a training team at an academy. I have never learned so much. The curriculum and the culture I inherited were steeped in tradition, and not the good kind. Over the years I was there, the content and delivery morphed and shifted. When I left, the training process looked nothing like what it had been when I arrived. I was proud of the progress, but the job was not finished. It should never be finished. If I walked back through those doors ten years from now, I would hope that the training would look unrecognizable to me.

Legacy is not about doing it the same way forever, or getting a drill named after you. Legacy is about leaving the jersey in a better place (Kerr, 2013). A law enforcement trainer's tremendous privilege and responsibility is to help prepare those entering the arena to prevail. We owe it to them to learn, grow, and get out of our comfort zone to serve them to the best of our ability.

- Leon

Sometimes the instructor, always the student.

For more information check out tfstraining.com

REFERENCES

Bibliography

Arnet, J. J., & Jensen, L. E. (2019). *Human development, a cultural approach.* Pearson.

Abdollahipour, R., Wulf, G., Psotta, R., & Palomo Nieto, M. (2015). Performance of gymnastics skills benefits from an external focus of attention. *Journal of Sports Sciences*, *33*(17), 1807–1813. https://doi.org/10.1080/02640414.2015.1012102

Alshak, M. N., & Das, J. M. (2023). Neuroanatomy, Sympathetic Nervous System. *StatPearls Publishing*, 5. https://www.ncbi.nlm.nih.gov/books/NBK542195/#

Applegate, R. (1976). *Kill or get killed: Riot control techniques, man handling and close combat.* Paladin Press.

Applegate, R., & Janich, M. D. (1998). *Bullseyes don't shoot back: The complete textbook of point shooting for close quarters combat.* Martial Blade Concepts LLC.

Artwohl, A., & Christensen, L. W. (1997). *Deadly force encounters: What cops need to know to mentally and physically prepare for and survive a gunfight*. Paladin Press.

Aslaksen, K., & Lorås, H. (2018). The modality-specific learning style hypothesis: A mini-review and implications for motor learning. *Frontiers in Psychology, 9*, 1538.

Askins, C. (1939). *The art of handgun shooting*. A.S. Barnes & Company.

Baldwin, S., Bennell, C., Blaskovits, B., Brown, A., Jenkins, B., Lawrence, C., McGale, H., Semple, T., & Andersen, J. P. (2022). A reasonable officer: Examining the relationships among stress, training, and performance in a highly realistic lethal force scenario. *Frontiers in Psychology, 12*, 759132. https://doi.org/10.3389/fpsyg.2021.759132

Battig, W. F. (1979). The flexibility of human memory. In L. S. Cermak & F. I. M. Craik (Eds.), *Levels of processing in human memory* (pp. 23-44). Lawrence Erlbaum Associates.

Beatty, J., & Lucero-Wagner, B. (2000). Handbook of Psychophysiology. Cambridge University Press.

Benarroch, E. E. (2014). Parasympathetic system: Overview. In *Encyclopedia of the neurological sciences* (pp. 805–808). Elsevier. https://doi.org/10.1016/B978-0-12-385157-4.00508-X

Bisley, J. W. (2020). Eye movement planning and control. In *The senses: A comprehensive reference* (pp. 465–471). Elsevier. https://doi.org/10.1016/B978-0-12-809324-5.24125-4

Bjork, R. A. (1994). Memory and metamemory considerations in the training of human beings. In J. Metcalfe & A. Shimamura (Eds.), *Metacognition: Knowing about knowing* (pp. 185–205). MIT Press.

Bjork, R. A., & Bjork, E. L. (2011). Making things hard on yourself, but in a good way: Creating desirable difficulties to enhance learning. In M. A. Gernsbacher, R. W. Pew, L. M. Hough, & J. R. Pomerantz (Eds.), *Psychology and the real world: Essays illustrating fundamental contributions to society* (pp. 56–64). Worth Publishers.

Bozeman, W. O., Quattrocchi, F. A., Winslow, J. E., III, Levine, S. D., & Fernandez, W. G. (2018). Injuries associated with police use of force. *Journal of Trauma and Acute Care Surgery*, *84*(3), 496–502. doi.org

Bradley, M. M., Miccoli, L., Escrig, M. A., & Lang, P. J. (2008). The pupil as a measure of emotional arousal and autonomic activation. *Psychophysiology*, *45*(4), 602–607. https://doi.org/10.1111/j.1469-8986.2008.00654.x

Carey, B. (2015). *How we learn: The surprising truth about when, where, and why it happens*. Random House.

Carretié, L. (2014). Exogenous (automatic) attention to emotional stimuli: A review. *Cognitive, Affective, & Behavioral Neuroscience, 14*(4), 1228–1258. https://doi.org/10.3758/s13415-014-0270-2

Cassidy, W. L. (1978). *Quick or dead: The rise and development of close-quarter combat firing of the self-loading pistol and other one-hand guns, with particular reference to prominent twentieth-century British and American methods of instruction* (1st ed.). Paladin Enterprises.

Cherry, E. C. (1953). Some experiments on the recognition of speech, with one and with two ears. *Journal of the Acoustical Society of America, 25*, 975–979. https://doi.org/10.1121/1.1907229

Chiodo, L. (2009). Winning a high-speed, close-distance gunfight. Paladin Press.

Christina, B., & Alpenfels, E. (2014). Influence of attentional focus on learning a swing path change. *International Journal of Golf Science, 3*, 35-49. https://doi.org/10.1123/ijgs.2014-0001

Cooper, D., Fuller, J., Wiggins, M. W., Wills, J. A., Main, L. C., & Doyle, T. (2024). Negative consequences of pressure on marksmanship may be offset by early training exposure to contextually relevant threat training: A systematic review and meta-analysis. *Human Factors: The Journal of the Human Factors and Ergonomics Society, 66*(1), 294–311. https://doi.org/10.1177/00187208211065907

Credland, A. G. (2006). Charles Random, Baron de Berenger, inventor,

marksman and proprietor of the Stadium. *Arms & Armour*, 3(2), 171–

191. https://doi.org/10.1179/174962606X136865

De Berenger, B. (1835). Helps and Hints to protect life and property. T. Hurst.

De Oca, B. M., & Black, A. A. (2013). Bullets versus burgers: Is it threat or

relevance that captures attention? *The American Journal of*

Psychology, *126*(3), 287–300.

https://doi.org/10.5406/amerjpsyc.126.3.0287

Donner, C. M., & Popovich, N. (2019). Hitting (or missing) the mark: An

examination of police shooting accuracy in officer-involved shooting

incidents. *Policing: An International Journal*, *42*(3), 474–489.

https://doi.org/10.1108/PIJPSM-05-2018-0060

Donovan, J. J., & Radosevich, D. J. (1999). A meta-analytic review of the

distribution of practice effect: Now you see it, now you don't. *Journal*

of Applied Psychology, 84(5), 795-805.

Drew, T., Võ, M. L.-H., & Wolfe, J. M. (2013). The invisible gorilla strikes again:

Sustained inattentional blindness in expert observers. *Psychological*

Science, 24(9), 1848–1853.

https://doi.org/10.1177/0956797613479386

Ericsson, K. A. (2008). Deliberate practice and acquisition of expert performance: A general overview. *Academic Emergency Medicine, 15*(11), 988-994.

Ericsson, K. A., Krampe, R. T., & Tesch-Römer, C. (1993). The role of deliberate practice in the acquisition of expert performance. *Psychological Review, 100*(3), 363–406. https://doi.org/10.1037/0033-295X.100.3.363

Fairbairn, W. E., Sykes, E. A., & Schwabe, R. (1942). *Shooting to live, with the one-hand gun.* Naval & Military Press, Ltd.

Federal Bureau of Investigation. (2025). *Law Enforcement Officers Killed and Assaulted, 1987-2023* [Dataset]. FBI.gov

Fitts, P. M., & Posner, M. I. (1967). *Human performance.* Brooks/Cole Publishing Company.

Fletcher, K., Neal, A., & Yeo, G. (2017). The effect of motor task precision on pupil diameter. *Applied Ergonomics, 65,* 309–315. https://doi.org/10.1016/j.apergo.2017.07.010

Fox, E., Griggs, L., & Mouchlianitis, E. (2007). The detection of fear-relevant stimuli: Are guns noticed as quickly as snakes? *Emotion, 7*(4), 691–696. https://doi.org/10.1037/1528-3542.7.4.691

Frazer, W. D. (2015). *American Pistol Shooting.* Skyhorse Publishing Company, Incorporated.

Green, M., & Odom, J. V. (Eds.). (2008). *Forensic vision with application to highway safety* (3rd ed.). Lawyers & Judges Publishing Company.

Graham v. Connor, 490 U.S. 386 (1989).

Greenwood, C. (1966). Police firearms training. *Journal of the Forensic Science Society*, *6*(3), 116–162. https://doi.org/10.1016/S0015-7368(66)70326-0

Hagan, M. A., Wong, Y. T., & Pesaran, B. (2020). Visual-motor integration in the primate brain. In *The senses: A comprehensive reference* (pp. 532–548). Elsevier. https://doi.org/10.1016/B978-0-12-809324-5.24265-X

Honig, A. (2008). A Survey of the Research on Human Factors Related to Lethal Force Encounters: Implications for Law Enforcement Training, Tactics, and Testimony. *Law Enforcement Executive Forum*, 8, 24.

Hopfinger, J. B., & Mangun, G. R. (2001). Electrophysiological studies of reflexive attention. In *Advances in psychology* (Vol. 133, pp. 3–26). Elsevier. https://doi.org/10.1016/S0166-4115(01)80003-0

Hung, G. K., Sun, L., Semmlow, J. L., & Ciuffreda, K. J. (1990). Suppression of sensitivity to change in target disparity during vergence eye movements. *Experimental Neurology*, *110*(3), 291–297. https://doi.org/10.1016/0014-4886(90)90041-P

Jordan, W. H. (1965). *No Second Place Winner*. W.H. Jordan

Kantor, M. A., Lewinski, W. J., Garg, H., Tenbrink, J., Lau, J., & Pettitt, R. W. (2022). Kinematic Analysis of Naive Shooters in Common Law Enforcement Encounters. Journal of Forensic Biomechanics, 13(5), 7.

Kantor, M. A., Reiner, S., & Pettitt, R. W. (2024). Evaluation of tactical movement and firearm draw performance during charging knife attacks. *Police Practice and Research*, *25*(1), 101–109. https://doi.org/10.1080/15614263.2023.2222872

Kerr, J. M. (2013). *Legacy: 15 lessons in leadership: what the All Blacks can teach about the business of life.* Constable.

Klein, C. (2004). *Instinct combat shooting: Defensive handgunning for police* (3rd ed.). Looseleaf Law Publications.

Koivisto, M., Hyönä, J., & Revonsuo, A. (2004). The effects of eye movements, spatial attention, and stimulus features on inattentional blindness. *Vision Research*, *44*(27), 3211–3221. https://doi.org/10.1016/j.visres.2004.07.026

Lavery, J. J., & Suddon, F. H. (1962). Retention of simple motor skills as a function of the number of trials by which KR is delayed. *Perceptual and Motor Skills, 15*(1), 231–237. https://doi.org/10.2466/pms.1962.15.1.231

Lee, T. D. (2011). *Motor control in everyday actions.* Human Kinetics.

Lee, T. D., & Magill, R. A. (1983). The locus of contextual interference in motor-skill acquisition. *Journal of Experimental Psychology: Learning, Memory, and Cognition, 9*(4), 730–746.

Lewinski, W. (2008). The attention study: A study on the presence of selective attention in firearms officers. *Law Enforcement Executive Forum*, 8(6), 107–139.

Lewinski, W., Avery, R., Dysterheft, J., Dicks, N. D., & Bushey, J. (2015). The real risks during deadly police shootouts: Accuracy of the naïve shooter. *International Journal of Police Science & Management*, 17(2), 117–127. https://doi.org/10.1177/1461355715582975

Lewinski, W., Dysterheft, J., Bushey, J., & Dicks, N. (2015). Ambushes leading cause of officer fatalities - when every second counts: Analysis of officer movement from trained ready tactical positions. *Law Enforcement Executive Forum*, 15(1), 1-16. https://doi.org/10.19151/LEEF.2015.1051a

Lewinski, W., Seefeldt, D., Redmann, C., Gonin, M., Sargent, S., Dysterheft, J., & Thiem, P. (2016). The speed of a prone subject. *Law Enforcement Executive Forum*, 16(1), 113-128. https://doi.org/10.19151/LEEF.2016.1601f

Lohse, K. R., Sherwood, D. E., & Healy, A. F. (2010). How changing the focus of attention affects performance, kinematics, and electromyography in dart throwing. *Human movement science, 29*(4), 542–555. https://doi.org/10.1016/j.humov.2010.05.001

Lundwall, R. A. (2023). Visual reflexive attention as a useful measure of development. *Frontiers in Psychology, 14*, 1206045. https://doi.org/10.3389/fpsyg.2023.1206045

Manning, K. (1986). Eye-movement-dependent loss in vision and its time course during vergence. *The Journal of Neuroscience, 6*(7), 1976–1982. https://doi.org/10.1523/JNEUROSCI.06-07-01976.1986

Manning, K. A., & Riggs, L. A. (1984). Vergence eye movements and visual suppression. *Vision Research, 24*(6), 521–526. https://doi.org/10.1016/0042-6989(84)90105-6

Massa, L. J., & Mayer, R. E. (2006). Testing the ATI hypothesis: Should multimedia instruction accommodate verbalizer-visualizer cognitive style? *Learning and Individual Differences, 16*(4), 321–335.

Mathôt, S. (2018). Pupillometry: Psychology, physiology, and function. *Journal of Cognition, 1*(1), 16. https://doi.org/10.5334/joc.18

Mays, L. E., & Gamlin, P. D. (1995). Neuronal circuitry controlling the near response. *Current Opinion in Neurobiology, 5*(6), 763–768. https://doi.org/10.1016/0959-4388(95)80104-9

McBride, D. M., Cutting, J. C., & Zimmerman, C. L. (2022). *Cognitive psychology: Theory, process, and methodology* (3rd ed.). SAGE Publications.

Memmert, D. (2006). The effects of eye movements, age, and expertise on inattentional blindness. *Consciousness and Cognition*, *15*(3), 620–627. https://doi.org/10.1016/j.concog.2006.01.001

Molina, S. L., Bott, T. S., & Stodden, D. F. (2019). Applications of the speed–accuracy trade-off and impulse-variability theory for teaching ballistic motor skills. *Journal of Motor Behavior*, *51*(6), 690–697. https://doi.org/10.1080/00222895.2019.1565526

Morrison, G. B. (1998). Police handgun qualification: Practical measure or aimless activity? *Policing: An International Journal of Police Strategies & Management*, *21*(3), 510–533.

Motlagh, M., & Geetha, R. (2022, November 15). Physiology, accommodation. In *StatPearls* [Internet]. StatPearl Publishing. https://www.ncbi.nlm.nih.gov/books/NBK542189/

Mroz, R. (2000). *Defensive shooting for real-life encounters: A critical look at current training methods*. Paladin Press.

National Law Enforcement Firearms Instructors Association. (2025). *Officer involved shootings with pistol red dot sights*. NLEFIA

O'Neal, B. (1983). *Encyclopedia of western gun-fighters* (1st ed., 3rd printing). University of Oklahoma Press.

O'Neill, J., Hartman, M. E., O'Neill, D. A., & Lewinski, W. J. (2018). Further analysis of the unintentional discharge of firearms in law enforcement. *Applied Ergonomics, 68,* 267–272. https://doi.org/10.1016/j.apergo.2017.12.004

Parr, R., & Button, C. (2009). End-point focus of attention: Learning the 'catch' in rowing. *International Journal of Sport Psychology, 40*(4), 616–635.

Pashler, H., McDaniel, M., Rohrer, D., & Bjork, R. (2008). Learning styles: Concepts and evidence. *Psychological Science in the Public Interest, 9*(3), 105-119.

Reppert, T. R., Rigas, I., Herzfeld, D. J., Sedaghat-Nejad, E., Komogortsev, O., & Shadmehr, R. (2018). Movement vigor as a traitlike attribute of individuality. *Journal of Neurophysiology, 120*(2), 741–757. https://doi.org/10.1152/jn.00033.2018

Roberts, D., & Bristow, A. (1969). *An introduction to modern police firearms.* Glencoe Press.

Robins, P., Tyler, N., & Child, P. R. (2005). *The legend of W.E. Fairbairn: Gentleman & warrior: The Shanghai years* (1st ed.). CQB Publications (UK).

Rohrer, D., & Pashler, H. (2012). Learning styles: where's the

evidence? *Medical education*, *46*(7), 634–635.

https://doi.org/10.1111/j.1365-2923.2012.04273.x

Schmidt, R. A., & Lee, T. D. (2019). *Motor learning and performance: From

principles to application* (6th ed.). Human Kinetics.

Schmidt, R. A., Lee, T. D., Winstein, C. J., Wulf, G., & Zelaznik, H. N. (2019).

Motor control and learning: A behavioral emphasis (Sixth edition).

Human Kinetics.

Scott, D. W. (2025). Officer involved shootings [Unpublished raw data]. MILO

Shea, J. B., & Morgan, R. L. (1979). Contextual interference effects on the

acquisition, retention, and transfer of a motor skill. *Journal of

Experimental Psychology: Human Learning and Memory, 5*(2), 179–

187.

Simons, D. J., & Chabris, C. F. (1999). Gorillas in our midst: Sustained

inattentional blindness for dynamic events. *Perception*, *28*(9), 1059–

1074.

Simons, D. J., & Schlosser, M. D. (2017). Inattentional blindness for a gun

during a simulated police vehicle stop. *Cognitive Research: Principles

and Implications*, *2*(1), 37. https://doi.org/10.1186/s41235-017-0074-3

Spaulding, D. (2024, March 26). *Front sight focus: Myth or mandatory?* Guns

and Ammo. https://www.gunsandammo.com/editorial/front-sight-

focus-myth-or-mandatory/494124#replay

Stephens, D. W. (2019). *Officer involved shootings: Incident executive

summary*. National Policing Institute.

Strayer, D. L., Drews, F. A., & Johnston, W. A. (2003). Cell phone-induced

failures of visual attention during simulated driving. *Journal of

Experimental Psychology: Applied, 9*(1), 23–32.

https://doi.org/10.1037/1076-898X.9.1.23

Swinnen, S. P., Schmidt, R. A., Nicholson, D. E., & Shapiro, D. C. (1990).

Information feedback for skill acquisition: Instantaneous knowledge of

results degrades learning. *Journal of Experimental Psychology:

Learning, Memory, and Cognition, 16*(4), 706–

716. https://doi.org/10.1037/0278-7393.16.4.706

Taubert, R. K. (2012). *Rattenkrieg! The art and science of close quarters battle

pistol* (1st edition). Saber Press.

Taylor, P. L. (2021). "Engineering resilience" into split-second shoot/no shoot

decisions: The effect of muzzle-position. *Police Quarterly, 24*(2), 185–

204. https://doi.org/10.1177/1098611120960688

Trujillo, N., Gómez, D., Trujillo, S., López, J. D., Ibáñez, A., & Parra, M. A. (2021). Attentional bias during emotional processing: Behavioral and electrophysiological evidence from an emotional flanker task. *PLOS ONE, 16*(4), e0249407. https://doi.org/10.1371/journal.pone.0249407

Tueller, D. (1983, March). How close is too close? *SWAT Magazine.*

Van Zoest, W., Van der Stigchel, S., & Donk, M. (2017). Conditional control in visual selection. *Attention, Perception, & Psychophysics, 79*(6), 1555–1572. https://doi.org/10.3758/s13414-017-1352-3

Vickers, J. N. (2007). *Perception, cognition, and decision training: The quiet eye in action.* Human Kinetics.

Vickers, J. N., & Lewinski, W. (2012). Performing under pressure: Gaze control, decision-making and shooting performance of elite and rookie police officers. *Human Movement Science, 31*(1), 101–117. https://doi.org/10.1016/j.humov.2011.04.004

Vila, B. J., & Morrison, G. B. (1994). Biological Limits To Police Combat Handgun Shooting Accuracy. *American Journal of Police*, 13(1), 30.

White, M. D. (2006). Hitting the target (or not): Comparing characteristics of fatal, injurious, and noninjurious police shootings. *Police Quarterly, 9*(3), 303–330. https://doi.org/10.1177/1098611105277199

Willingham, D. T., Hughes, E. M., & Dobolyi, D. G. (2015). The scientific status of learning styles theories. *Teaching of Psychology, 42*(3), 266–271.

Winstein, C. J., & Schmidt, R. A. (1990). Reduced frequency of knowledge of

  results enhances motor skill learning. *Journal of Experimental*

  Psychology: Learning, Memory, and Cognition, 16(4), 677–

  691. https://doi.org/10.1037/0278-7393.16.4.677

Wulf, G., & Shea, C. H. (2004). Understanding the role of augmented feedback:

  The good, the bad, and the ugly. In A. M. Williams & N. J. Hodges

  (Eds.), *Skill acquisition in sport: Research, theory and practice* (pp.

  121–144). Routledge.

Wulf, G., Höß, M., & Prinz, W. (1998). Instructions for motor learning:

  differential effects of internal versus external focus of attention. *Journal*

  of Motor Behavior, 30(2), 169–179.

  https://doi.org/10.1080/00222899809601334

Zachry, T., Wulf, G., Mercer, J., & Bezodis, N. (2005). Increased movement

  accuracy and reduced EMG activity as the result of adopting an

  external focus of attention. *Brain research bulletin, 67*(4), 304–309.

  https://doi.org/10.1016/j.brainresbull.2005.06.035

Table of Figures